W9-BAI-198

EAU CLAIRE DISTRICT LIBRARY

*
641.8
G

11,243

Good Housekeeping
Good Housekeeping Complete
book of cake decorating

EAU CLAIRE DISTRICT LIBRARY

EAU CLAIRE DISTRICT LIBRARY

Good Housekeeping
Complete Book of
Cake Decorating

*
641.8
G.

Baker M Taylor - 1/24/74 - 7.93

Good Housekeeping Complete Book of Cake Decorating

EAU CLAIRE DISTRICT LIBRARY

GOOD HOUSEKEEPING BOOKS

73129

11,243

Color photographs by JAMES VILES, PAUL DOME, HI WILLIAMS, and HERBERT MATTER

Copyright © MCMLXI, MCMLXXIII by The Hearst Corporation.

Manufactured in the United States of America. No part of this book may be reproduced in any manner whatsoever without the written permission of the publisher. ISBN 0–87851–012–5. Library of Congress Catalog Number 73–83959.

CONTENTS

FOREWORD

The expression of one's love and interest and desire to give takes many forms. Great artists sing or paint or write; architects send buildings soaring skyward; scientists work toward great discoveries that will benefit mankind. Each gives according to his own measure.

This book is a tribute to the thousands of homemakers who find in cake decorating their own expression of that same love and interest and desire to give. Their letters to us, often including photographs of their finished triumphs, testify to the happiness this art adds to their lives. Through these letters we glimpse, as well, the sparkle it brings to their children's eyes and the joy it gives to grown-ups too. Who *doesn't* like to have a special cake made in his own special honor?

There are numerous authors of this book, headed, of course by our food editors, past and present, and their staffs. And we cannot omit our readers, who have shared their ideas with us and have encouraged us, by their letters, to go on and on in the development of recipes and techniques. It is our great hope that the pages that follow will furnish inspiration for saying "Love and Best Wishes" on many memorable occasions.

WILLIE MAE ROGERS
Director
Good Housekeeping Institute

Cake Decorating Is Fun I

Before You Decorate The Cake

We've yet to meet anyone, young or old, who doesn't love celebrating a special occasion with a wonderful, fanciful cake—the kind that's so pretty or so gay you almost hate to cut it. And if you think that making these attractive confections requires the skill of a caterer, you're wrong. The delightful examples in this collection were created in GOOD HOUSE-KEEPING's kitchens, later duplicated by pleasantly surprised homemakers. While a few of our cakes took a bit of time, not a single one was truly hard to make. So even if you are a novice, you can duplicate the same impressive results—if you just follow our instructions.

Choose the cake you want to make from the recipes found in this book. Then assemble the equipment and the ingredients needed; make sure your working space is in order.

General Instructions:

For a light, high cake simply follow a few rules: Be sure to measure accurately, use the method of mixing ingredients and of properly baking the batter that the recipe specifies, and use only the best ingredients available. Cool the cake on wire racks *thoroughly* before frosting.

Types of Cakes:

There are really only two different types of cakes—butter- and sponge-type cakes. Cakes that contain shortening are called butter-type cakes. Those that rely on beaten egg whites for leavening are called sponge-type cakes. Within each of these cake categories we have a great many variations. Butter cakes are sometimes called plain cakes and are made by either the conventional (creaming butter and sugar together) or one-bowl method. Angel food cake

is the most popular in the sponge-type group, which also includes sponge and chiffon cakes.

To Make a Good Cake:

It is wise to assemble all equipment necessary before beginning the actual measuring or mixing. Place all ingredients on work surface and allow them to come to room temperature.

Use only standard measuring cups and spoons. You'll need two standard cups, one for dry ingredients, the other for liquids. A standard measuring cup holds 8 oz. and is marked on one side to show ¼, ½, and ¾ cup, and on the other side to show ⅓ and ⅔ cup. The liquid measuring cup extends above the 1-cup line so you can measure without spilling. When it is made of glass you can see to measure the liquid right on the line.

A set of graduated measuring cups is convenient for measuring and leveling part-cup amounts. These come in 1, ½, ⅓, and ¼ cup sizes.

A set or two of standard measuring spoons is a necessity; these include 1 tablespoon, 1 teaspoon, ½ teaspoon, and ¼ teaspoon. Use the tablespoon for measuring less than ¼ cup amounts.

You will also need a spatula or straight-edged knife for leveling measurements, a large spoon for spooning ingredients into measuring cups, a rubber scraper to clean out measuring cup or spoon and to use while mixing.

Next read the cake recipe all the way through. Then follow directions exactly; otherwise the best recipe can go wrong.

Use pans that are the exact size and depth indicated. Bigger, smaller, or shallower pans than those called for can cause a cake to fail.

Be sure metal cake pans are bright and shiny inside and out, so cakes will brown evenly, delicately. Dull, dark pans cause cake to brown too fast, too unevenly. To keep cake pans shiny, clean with steel-wool soap pads.

Follow the recipe exactly. No substitutions

of ingredients, no changes in amounts, no changes in directions should be made.

Never double or halve a cake recipe; this usually means trouble. It takes a little longer, but you will be sure of the results, if you make up the exact recipe as many times as needed.

Use the exact ingredients called for — double-acting baking powder, cake flour, etc. This can mean the difference between a masterpiece and a mediocrity. Bake cake at the temperature and for the time period specified.

Do These Little Jobs Before You Mix a Cake:

If cake pans are to be lined with paper, set the pan on a large piece of waxed paper. Trace around bottom of pan with point of scissors or sharp knife. Cut out; place in bottom of cake pan. Paper should fit snugly. Making several liners at once saves time. You can also buy cake liners, already cut.

If cake pans are to be greased, apply thin film of salad oil or soft shortening with paper or pastry brush.

If pans are to be lined with waxed paper, they should be greased before placing paper in pans unless directed otherwise.

If cake pans are to be floured, sprinkle each greased pan with a little flour; then shake pan to coat it evenly. Remove excess flour by gently tapping inverted pan on work surface.

Start heating oven in time to have it heated to specified temperature when cake batter is ready—this usually takes 10 to 15 min.

Chop nuts, prepare fruit, etc., ahead.

Most Cake Troubles Can Be Traced To:

Not using ingredients called for. Substitutes are not the same, even though they may look so.

Not using accurate, level measurements. Small variations in amounts of ingredients may affect volume, texture, or crust.

Not baking in right pan, at right temperature, for right time.

Be careful not to over- or under-beat cake batter. Beat for only the time specified or to the described state for the batter. Either underbeating or overbeating batter can cause cake failure.

Always use the best ingredients possible when making a cake. Be sure to use the kind of shortening called for in the recipe. Whatever the shortening, in cakes made by the conventional method, it should be beaten with the sugar until light and fluffy, almost like whipped cream. In the one-bowl method cakes, the shortening, plus part or all of the liquid, is added directly to the sifted dry ingredients before beating.

Use the type of flour specified in the recipe —no other. All our cake recipes call for flour sifted just before measuring. When measuring sifted flour, spoon it lightly into the measuring cup, scraping the top level with a spatula or straight-edged knife. Then resift again with baking powder and salt, or as recipe directs.

To measure granulated sugar, spoon it lightly into measuring cup and level off with spatula or straight-edged knife.

To measure brown sugar, pack it firmly into the cup using back of spoon. When turned out it should hold the shape of the cup.

In the case of baking powder, use the type specified in our recipe, and, of course, measure it level.

Baking the Cake:

Just before you start mixing your cake, start heating the oven so it will be at indicated temperature when cake is ready to be baked.

In pouring batter into lightly greased and floured pans, or into pans lined with waxed paper, spread it evenly with rubber spatula, beginning in the center and spreading to edge of pan. If sponge-type cake, cut through batter several times to remove air bubbles. If making separate layers, divide the batter evenly (a scale, if you have one, is ideal for this purpose) so layers will be uniform.

In placing the pans in preheated oven, make sure they do not touch; air must circulate around each pan. Cakes may be baked on both oven racks at the same time, if they are placed diagonally. Opening the oven door prior to minimum baking time is unwise because it may cause a cake failure.

When minimum baking time is up, peek in oven and lightly touch center of cake. If cake springs back and no imprint remains, it's done. For a double check, insert cake tester or toothpick—it must be clean when you remove it for cake to be done.

Make it a practice to have your oven temperature control checked periodically. Too slow an oven may cause the cake to rise and then fall, producing a heavy, coarse cake. Too hot an oven may cause the cake surface to break and have a cracked appearance and usually a hump, too.

After removing a butter-type cake from the

8

oven, let it stand in the pan on a wire cake rack about 10 min., so cake will leave sides of pan freely and will be less likely to break. Then carefully remove cake from pan and finish cooling on rack.

After removing a sponge-type cake from the oven, invert pan and let cake hang in pan until it is cold. Now insert spatula directly against pan, then pull it out. Repeat around edges and tube. Then invert cake on rack and lift off pan. For high, fluffy wedges in sponge-type cakes, pull pieces apart with cake breaker or two forks.

Don't fail to refer to each cake recipe and to follow its directions closely.

Making a Cake from a Mix:

Today's homemaker is blessed in having a wonderful variety of cake mixes with which to tempt her family. Whichever cake mix is your choice, do read and follow the cake-mix directions to the letter.

Do preheat the oven, and never sift a cake mix. If it calls for water, use water. If it calls for milk, use milk; *don't substitute* one for the other. Do mix exactly as the label directs; don't skimp on beating time. Do use the exact pan sizes called for on the label; changes in the pan sizes may mean failure for the cake. Don't overbake the cake, either; test for doneness when minimum time is up. Don't experiment! Play safe, use only the variations on the package.

Frosting the Cake

Even the simplest cake becomes a wonderful treat when it's attractively frosted. One thing to remember is that frosting is always at its best the day it goes on the cake, although many frostings may stay fresh for several days. Never start to make the frosting until you have read the recipe from beginning to the end; and do be careful about measurements.

Frostings generally fall into one of these three categories: uncooked or butter cream, cooked fudge, and fluffy cooked frostings.

General Pointers on Making Uncooked Frosting:

1. Have shortening at room temperature. Butter may be substituted for part of shortening if butter flavor is desired; however, the frosting will not be as white as when shortening only is used, and it will be a bit softer.

2. If mixing ingredients in electric mixer, use low speed to avoid whipping air into the frosting; it should not be aerated at all; rather, it should be very smooth.

3. When frosting is mixed, put it in a container that can be tightly closed. If air is kept from the frosting it will remain smooth. Store container in a cool place—do not refrigerate unless kitchen is quite hot—then frosting will always be ready to use.

4. After you remove some of frosting from the container, be sure to re-cover the container at once, so frosting will remain smooth.

5. A good uncooked frosting has these qualities: a fine flavor; creamy, glossy texture; uncracked appearance when cut.

General Pointers on Making Cooked Frosting:

1. Be sure that beater and bowls are free from grease.

2. Have egg whites at room temperature before using. This makes for greater volume.

3. Separate whites from yolks carefully so that not even a speck of yolk is in whites.

4. Cook frosting as recipe directs. If it says "Cook over boiling water" be sure water is boiling.

5. A cooked frosting should be cooled slightly before using, or it will soak into the cake.

6. A good cooked frosting has these qualities: an uncracked glossy exterior; soft delicate texture; a well-blended flavor; a fluffy exterior.

Frostings You Buy:

Packaged frosting mixes and canned ready-to-spread frostings may be substituted for some of the frosting recipes in this book. For example, packaged fluffy white frosting mix may be used in place of any foamy-type frosting (such as boiled or seven-minute frostings) made with beaten egg whites and sugar. And packaged and canned ready-to-spread frostings in various flavors may be substituted for homemade ones calling for shortening, confectioners' sugar and liquid. Check the yield on the package or can label to be sure you'll have enough to frost the cake and to allow for any decorating called for.

How to Fill and Frost Cake:

Square, Loaf, Sheet, or Tube Cake (your own or bakers')

1. Cool cake well. Brush or rub off loose crumbs; trim ragged edges with scissors.

2. Place cake, with top side up (if tube cake, place bottom side up), on flat cake plate or tray that extends about 2″ beyond the cake.

3. To keep cake plate clean while frosting cake, cover outer area of plate with strips of waxed paper, extending them beyond edge of plate.

4. So cake can be turned as you frost, set cake plate on mixing bowl, with plate extending at least 1″ beyond rim of bowl.

5. Use a large spatula to spread frosting.

6. Working quickly, first frost the entire cake with a thin, smooth layer of frosting; this holds down the crumbs. Then, working quickly, refrost sides of cake first, using upward strokes.

7. Pile rest of frosting on top; spread out in attractive swirls to meet sides. Spread naturally and irregularly, not painfully smooth.

8. Let frosting set slightly; then carefully pull out waxed-paper strips.

Layer Cake
(your own or bakers')

1. If there is any difference between layers, make thicker layer the bottom layer; use smooth-crusted layer on top. Place first layer, upside down, on cake plate. Adjust strips of waxed paper on plate, as in step 3, above.

2. Spread filling on bottom layer, almost to edge (if filling is soft, spread only to 1″ from edge). Adjust second layer, with top side up, so edges are even and cake is of uniform height.

3. If top layer slides, insert wire cake tester or slender knitting needle through both layers to anchor them. (Remove tester or needle before frosting top of cake.) Then frost cake, as in steps 4 to 8, above.

When Coloring Frosting:

There are two forms of food color on the market today—liquid and paste. Liquid food color is available at most supermarkets in bottles or plastic tubes; it comes in four basic colors: red, yellow, blue, and green. From these basic colors it is possible to make many other colors. For example:

Orange—3 drops red and 5 drops yellow
Violet—1 drop red and 2 drops blue
Brown—4 drops yellow, 1 drop green, 3 drops red

Peach—2 drops red and 5 drops yellow
Lime—3 drops yellow and 1 drop green
Strawberry—5 drops red and 3 drops yellow
For additional color blends, check package labels.

Paste food color comes in a very wide range of colors, is somewhat more expensive than liquid color, and may be purchased from a supply house.*

In using food color it is always advisable to use a relatively small amount, for a little goes a long way. To add liquid food color to white frosting, shake, or add it with a toothpick, a few drops at a time.

To add paste color to white frosting, spoon a little of the frosting away from the rest in the bowl. With toothpick place a small amount of paste color on spatula; then thoroughly mix color into frosting on side of bowl, adding more color if necessary to obtain a shade slightly darker than the desired color. Now blend the colored frosting with the white frosting until color is even throughout.

Generally speaking you'll find it easier to duplicate the colors found in nature than to reproduce such colors as black or gray.

How to Tint Coconut:

Flaked or fine grated coconut, delicately colored, is fun to use and quick to do. Color coconut this way: Blend 1 teasp. milk or water with a drop or so of desired food color. Add 1½ cups flaked coconut, also a little peppermint, almond, or vanilla extract, if desired. Toss with fork until blended.

How to Toast Coconut:

Spread coconut out thinly in shallow pan. Place in 350° F. oven to toast until delicately browned, stirring coconut or shaking pan often to toast evenly.

Decorating the Cake

Everyone is enchanted by decorated cakes! In this book we teach you how to decorate cakes of many kinds for your own satisfaction and the joy of others. It is easy and fun, though in some instances time consuming, but we are sure you will find it well worth the effort involved.

* See p. 179.

*Decorating Tubes:

To help all of you, and especially those of you who are beginners, each of our decorated cake recipes in this book not only indicates the frosting which should be used in decorating it, but the tube or tubes which will be needed in accomplishing this.

On p. 13 to 23 you can see just what each decorating tube looks like, and what sort of a design it makes.

*Decorating Bags:

As for the decorating bag which holds both the frosting and the decorating tubes, you have a choice here, as well.

You can cut your own or buy pre-cut parchment paper triangles, and then quickly roll them into decorating bags or cones, as shown on p. 23. These are especially nice when you are going to be using several colors in decorating a cake—one color in each cone. And, of course, they can be discarded after use.

Or you may prefer the relatively new, transparent plastic bags which are durable and flexible and may be re-used a number of times after washing. They are 9″ long, come in sets of four, and are exciting to use because you can see the frosting and so watch your progress.

Then there are plastic-coated decorating bags which are waterproof, stay pliable, are easy to wash, and dry, and come in a number of lengths. They last indefinitely.

*Cake Decorating Sets:

Or your choice may be one of the cake decorating sets — either a metal decorating syringe, or a plastic-coated bag, along with a group of the most often used tubes and a standard coupling with which to attach each tube to the bag. And once you've passed the beginner stage, you'll probably not be able to resist a set of the 26 or 52 most often used tubes, specially boxed, with each tube on its own knob so its design can be easily identified.

* Colored Frostings in Plastic Tubes:

For some of your cake decorations, you may wish to use the colored frostings that come in plastic tubes. You buy these at the grocer's, in the following colors: red, blue, yellow, green, and pink. They require no refrigeration

* See p. 179.

and are ready to use just as they come from the tubes. No decorating frosting to make!

You may also buy plastic tubes or tips that screw on the tops of these frosting tubes for making leaves, roses, rosettes or stars and doing writing. A flower nail is included, too. These plastic tips are sold wherever the frosting is sold, come in a small cellophane bag, and are moderately priced.

* Decorating Jelly or gel:

This is also available at the grocer's and comes in small plastic tubes in the following colors: pink, red, blue, yellow, green, white; brown and orange in fall. It's fine for doing writing, outlining, etc., on the cake.

Spatulas:

A small thin spatula is a must in cake decorating, for swirling the frosting on the cake and for putting the frosting into the decorating bag. A blade of 6¼″ by 1″ is just right. Have two of them if you can.

*Flower Nails:

The flower nail is an alternate for the small covered jar top on which our Susan makes her posies, p. 28. If you prefer to use such a nail, get several. They come in metal or plastic, some having wide heads, some round, some flat, some concave, depending on the depth of the flower you're making.

*Decorating Comb:

This little aluminum gadget gives a finished look to a cake in a matter of minutes. Resembling a comb, it makes close parallel lines around the side or across the top of the cake merely by being drawn lightly through the frosting.

* Cake Decorating Stencils:

These come in plastic or heavy waxed cardboard and may be used again and again. The stencil is held over frosted cake top and the spaces are filled in with very thin colored icing; or you may use a fine brush to apply the color, or sprinkle colored sugar through the stencil. These stencils come in various patterns: a rose, turkey, tree, heart, wreath, bell, lettering that says Happy Birthday, Merry Christmas, etc.

* See p. 179.

11

Cake Cutting

To Cut an Angel, Chiffon or Sponge Cake:

For fluffy high wedges, gently pull pieces apart with a cake breaker or two forks. Or saw off pieces with a sharp serrated or scalloped-edge knife.

To Cut a Layer or Loaf Cake:

Use a thin, pointed, very sharp knife. Insert the point of the knife into the cake and, keeping the point angled down slightly, *saw* through the cake *gently* back and forth. If frosting sticks to the knife, dip knife in hot water before cutting another slice.

To Cut Cakes to Best Advantage:

Especially when cakes are being cut for large groups, it is nice to know of the diagrammed ways, shown below. Broken lines show first cuts to be made.

To Freeze Cakes

Angel food, chiffon, sponge and butter cakes, or poundcakes or fruitcakes—any type or flavor, in fact—will freeze well. Loaf, layer, and cupcakes all freeze well, too. Just make and bake cakes as usual, then wrap whole or in portions. Set each cake on cardboard covered with foil or saran; wrap in freezer wrapping, then seal with freezer tape.

Cakes may be frozen frosted or unfrosted, but they keep longer and in better condition unfrosted. Butter and penuche-type frostings are best for freezing. Use part honey or corn syrup in penuche type, to prevent cracking. If a frosted cake is to be frozen, freeze the cake before wrapping it.

Unfrosted cake will keep up to 6 months at zero degrees; frosted, up to 3 months.

To thaw frosted cakes and cupcakes, unwrap them; leave unfrosted cakes wrapped. Thaw at room temperature, on cake rack. Cupcakes will thaw in about 30 min., cake layers in 1 hr., whole cakes in 2 or 3 hr. When thoroughly defrosted, frost as desired, following How to Fill and Frost Cake, p. 9.

To Pack a Cake for Traveling

Use a frosting that dries hard. Set cake on wooden board, then place in corrugated box of exact size of board. Lightly pack with crushed paper towels or tissue paper. Tie securely; carry upright.

If transporting cake in a car, set finished cake on large metal tray. Place a piece of wood same size as tray on back seat of car. Use blocks of wood to keep it level. Wet a large newspaper, wring out excess water. Press onto board, then set metal tray on top of it. Drive slowly and carefully; don't make any sudden stops.

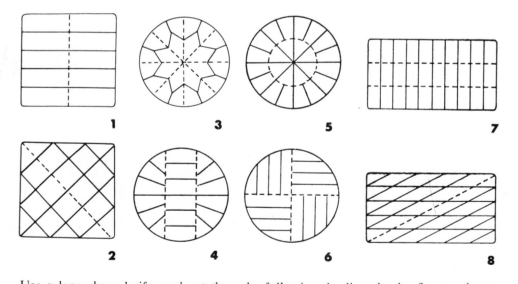

Use a long sharp knife, and cut the cake following the lines in the figures above.
For a square cake, use Figure 1 or 2.
For a layered cake use Figure 3, 4, 5 or 6.
For an oblong cake use Figure 7 or 8.

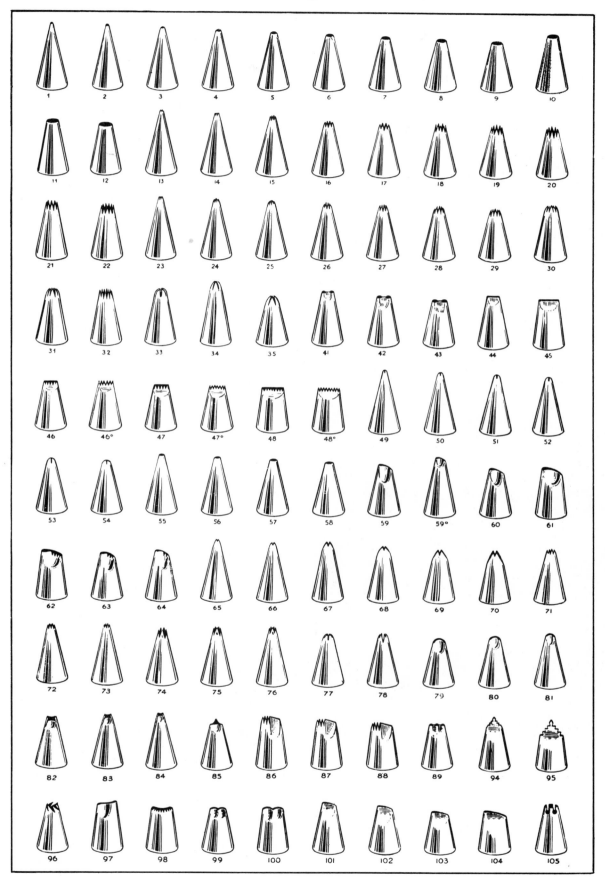

What They Do

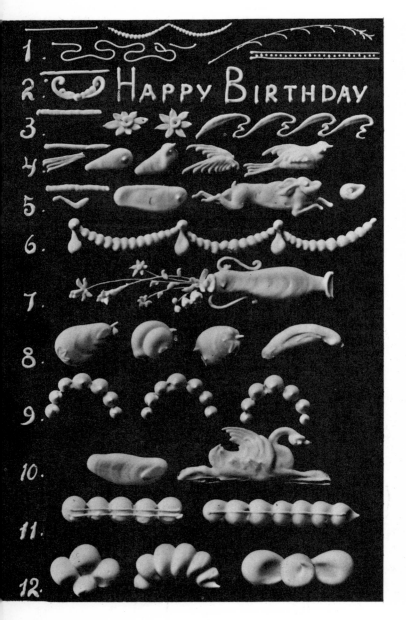

PLAIN TUBES

No. 1. Makes lines, fine stems, scrolls, vines, stamens on large flowers, little stamens in lilies of the valley. Most adaptable for fine writing.

No. 2. Fine for small lettering and writing, also for making the green balls which form center of wild rose, apple blossom, poinsettia.

No. 3. Makes thicker scrolls, puts finishing dots in fantasy flowers on cup cakes, and makes tiny buds for lilies of the valley and lilac sprays.

No. 4. Used for stems on flowers, heavy writing, the popular dove, etc.

No. 5. A favorite for making a number of borders, as well as bunnies, writing.

No. 6. Makes most attractive side borders. For the one shown, hold tube at angle. Start with a small bead, gradually increasing size of beads until center is reached; then decrease size to match first side; don't draw tube away until each section is finished.

No. 7. Nice tube for making vases; base and handles are done with tube no. 2; stems of the dainty flowers with tube no. 1.

No. 8. Popular for making loops, in contrasting color, on side of a cake. Also used to make many fruits such as pears, apples, peaches, bananas; no. 2 tube is used for their stems.

No. 9. Use instead of tube no. 8 if you desire decoration of larger size.

No. 10. Fine for making swans. Use tube no. 10 for his body. Change to tube no. 3 for neck and head, letting these flow out of body. Pipe on left wing, then make right wing somewhat smaller so left one is not hidden. Finish by piping on tail, with a few curved, upward strokes. A few choppy strokes around swan give effect of water.

No. 11. A number of borders can be made with this tube. First one shown is made by holding tube upright and having beads very close together. For second border, hold tube at an angle and do not withdraw it until entire border is made. Make thread line across beads with tube no. 1.

No. 12. Exceptionally good tube for decorating small iced cakes, petits-fours, etc.

14

OPEN STAR TUBES

No. 13. Makes pipings, straight and curved lines, scrolls, etc.

No. 14. Makes dainty fantasy flowers, lovely on small cup cakes, especially in a motif of pastel colors.

No. 15. Unusually good border tube. Start border with light pressures, moving tube up and down to get fancy effect. Enlarge design gradually by increasing pressure very slowly. This enlarges crinkled part.

No. 16. This is a six-point star tube which makes a very realistic pineapple. For the leaves, use the smallest leaf tube, no. 65; start making them at top of pineapple by using slight pressure and drawing up tube about ½". For base of pineapple run tube back and forth at least twice.

No. 17. Use a wavy motion with this tube and you'll get the attractive crinkled border shown. Diminishing the pressure makes it taper to a curved line at the end. Make the scroll with a no. 3 tube, overpiping it a number of times to prevent too flat an effect. Add beads in each center as shown.

No. 18. An extremely popular tube that lends itself easily to up-and-down motion and simple, interesting designs.

Nos. 19, 20, 21. These tubes graduate in size and are fascinating for making eight-point stars and interesting motifs on the side of a cake. A contrasting colored dot in the center of each star is worth trying.

No. 22. This nine-pointed tube makes a very wide scroll and is fine for shaping macaroons, dessert topping, whipped cream, meringue, potato borders, etc.

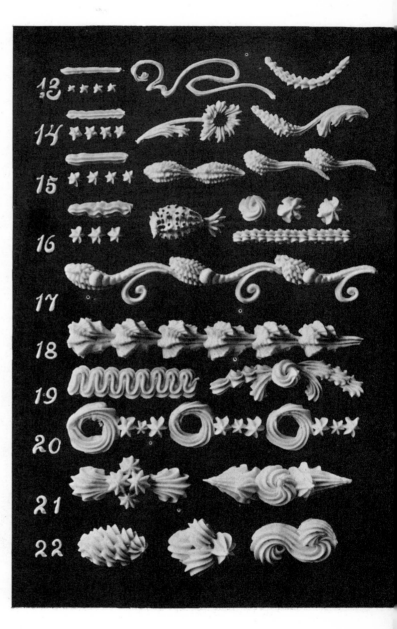

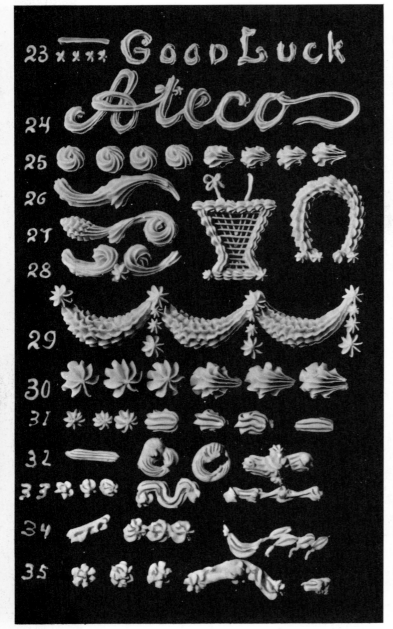

CLOSED STAR TUBES

These tubes run from no. 23 to 35, inclusive. The variety of stars, shells, writing and lettering that may be made from these tubes is surprising. The variations in style and size offer the decorator a fascinating scope for her originality.

Nos. 23 and 24 tubes are five-point stars which both write and print very expertly.

Nos. 25 and 26 are six-point stars which make delightful tiny rosettes, borders, designs, shells, garlands, etc. In making stars, keep them evenly spaced to insure their being shapely, with both sides of same size.

No. 27 is a seven-point star and is popular for making simple baskets, like that shown. The outlining border of the baskets is made with tube no. 27; the center latticework is made with tube no. 2.

No. 28 is an eight-point star and makes a lovely design for the side of a cake. First pipe the design shown, then overpipe once, completing the motif; be sure to diminish the flow of frosting at the end. Join every two motifs by placing a star between.

Nos. 29 and 30 are eight-point stars which make most attractive borders of stars, shells, garlands, etc., as pictured.

Nos. 31, 32, 33, 34, 35 are larger star tubes that lend themselves to the making of important-looking borders. No. 32 tube is fine for decorating deviled eggs. It also can be used for stuffed celery.

Incidentally, by using stars of different sizes in pastel colors a lovely border or beveled effect can be made.

16

DOUBLE LINE TUBES

Nos. 41, 42, 43. These double-line tubes are used when accurate spacing and double lines are required, as in parallel lines, crisscross patterns, and lattice patterns. The sizes are small, medium, and large, respectively, and they are especially convenient when finishing baskets and doing scroll work.

PLAIN AND FANCY RIBBON TUBES

Plain and fancy ribbon tubes run from Nos. 44 to 48°, as shown, and suggest great fun for everyone.

No. 44 is a flat tube created for making bows on bouquets or for borders which are made by holding the tube flat and moving it from side to side with a wavy motion.

No. 45 is a larger tube than no. 44. Motifs made with it may be in any pastel shade and will have very special appeal if overpiped with a fine white line, made with tube no. 1. The designs shown will suggest other attractive motifs to you.

No. 46 has serrations on one side, and tube no. 46° has serrations on both sides. So you may make either the flat fancy ribbon (with serrations on one side) or the closely crinkled ribbon which is made with an up-and-down movement of the hand.

No. 47. If you wish the border on your cake to be a little wider, use tube no. 47, as this tube is an eighth of an inch larger in size than tube no. 46.

No. 48° is the largest serrated tube and is often used for making bowknots which appear to tie together a bouquet of flowers for decoration on top of a cake. It is also very popular for making fancy ribbons and for the wicker and crossline designs that make basket work so interesting.

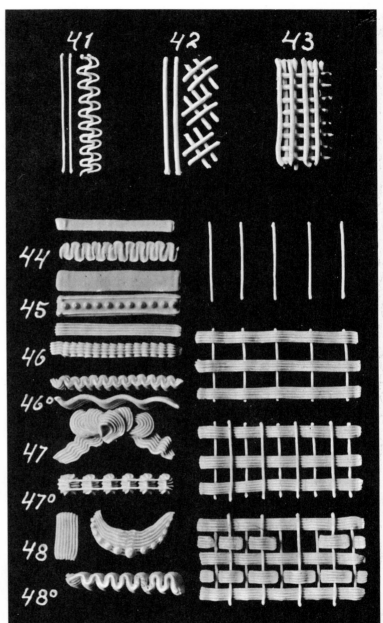

17

ASTER TUBES

The aster tubes come in six sizes, the smallest tube being no. 49, the largest, no. 54; the colors of the asters may vary from white or pink to violet or purple. Aster tubes may also be used for writing, lettering, and the making of small buds.

No. 53 makes a nice, simple scroll, good for beginners.

No. 54 makes another good design—especially so if you use tube no. 1 with contrasting colors to pipe the threads and join the two lines.

OVAL TUBES

Nos. 55, 56, 57 and 58 belong in the oval-tube group. They make interesting scrolls, borders, various flowers such as Easter lilies or stems, etc. These little motifs may be used to decorate petits-fours on French pastry.

FLOWER TUBES

No. 59. This is the tube making five-petal apple blossoms, with a delicate pink or white frosting or with two tones of pink. Have the deeper color on the wide side of the tube. Finish the center with five dark-brown dots.

No. 59°. This is a dahlia tube; note the progressive steps in the making of a dahlia as shown.

No. 60. This is primarily a pansy tube, although we also use much larger tubes to make this flower. Some pansies have three petals at top and two at bottom, and many vice-versa.

No. 61. This versatile little tube can be used for making a small rose or the open or wild rose.

18

FANCY BORDER TUBES

Many decorated cakes, regardless of how elaborate or simple they may be, have a finishing touch we call the border at their base. Here are three sizes of tubes for such borders—nos. 62, 63 and 64.

No. 62. This tube makes an interesting border, suitable for a large cake.

No. 63. This tube is a bit smaller than tube no. 62 and its border is finished with a wavy piping just below the last ridge on the flat line.

No. 64. This border is made by holding tube no. 64 practically flat on the cake and moving it slowly from side to side. This pipes a crinkled line. On top of this, pipe a flat even line just below the ridge. Now hold tube at a slight angle and pipe one more line over the preceding two, making it stand up, slightly tilted.

LEAF TUBES

The leaf tubes include nos. 65, 66, 67, 68, 69 and 70. No. 65, 66 and 67 tubes make tiny to somewhat larger leaves and borders as illustrated. Nos. 68, 69 and 70 make larger leaves. To create a standing leaf, hold tube almost perpendicular.

COMBINATION LEAF-AND-BORDER TUBES

No. 71. This tube is different on each side. To make an attractive leaf, with a ridge down the center, use tube with center seam upward.

Or, for an attractive border, turn tube seam side down, and use with a side-to-side wavy motion. Then, with a no. 1 or no. 2 tube, and a different color icing, you may go over these lines, creating a nice contrast.

No. 72. This tube makes a smaller replica of the designs made with tube no. 71. When using it for a border, make center line straight, in a contrasting color. The two crinkled leaves shown are linked together with a circlet, made with plain tube no. 2.

No. 73. This, the smallest of the combination leaf-and-border tubes, is generally used for a fine garland border. The scallops of these garlands are joined by the leaf motif, made with the other side of the tube. We suggest that you use a pale green icing for the leaf and any pastel shade of your choice for the border.

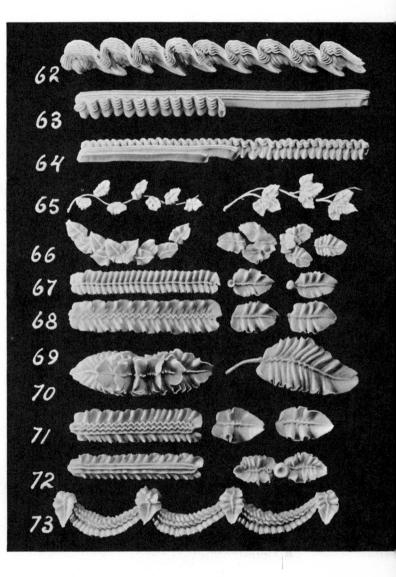

19

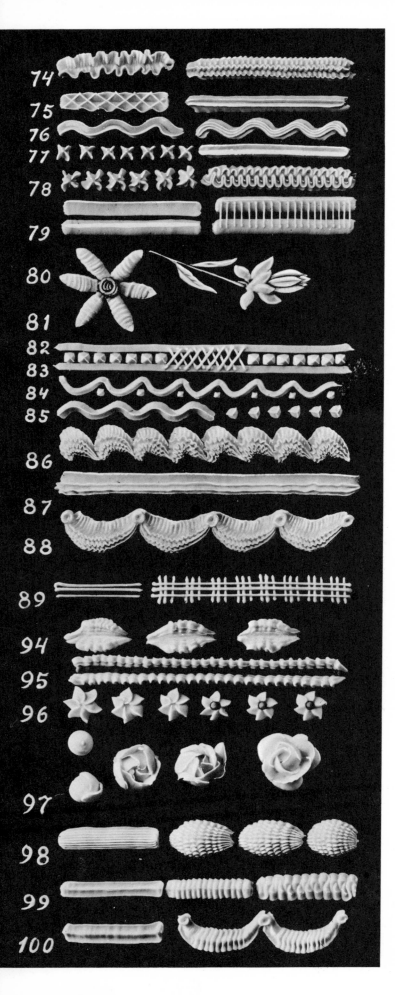

COMBINATION LEAF-AND-BORDER TUBES
(*continued*)

No. 74. (large) and no. 75 (medium) are the same tube, but 74 is larger. It is another combination leaf-and-border tube, with a different design on each side. By using it, seam side down, and making a side-to-side wavy motion, the design will resemble the fluting shown. By turning the tube around, and using the same motion, a tiny crinkly design will appear, resembling gathers.

No. 75 (medium). One size smaller than tube no. 74, this tube lends itself to a rather unusual border, no. 1 tube being used for the thread work. Then, by turning tube no. 75 directly around, a series of straight lines are made.

No. 76. This little tube, the same in make and design, is used for delightful little scallops which furnish a lane for a contrasting color.

No. 78. This tube is used primarily to make fantasy flowers, which are really little buds with centers filled with color. It may be used for delicate borders if held either at an angle or in a vertical position.

FLOWER TUBES

No. 79. This tube, also tubes no. 80 and 81, are used to create daffodils, narcissus, lilies of of the valley, a group of fantasy flowers, etc. In picture opposite you see two simple, quick border-design lines. The upper line is concave, made by holding tube with seam down. The lower line is convex, made by holding tube in reverse position.

For a really attractive design that's quick and simple, make a border of two convex lines, then fill with piped thread work, using a no. 2 plain tube and contrasting colors, as shown.

No. 80 and 81. To make the fantasy flower

shown at left in this illustration, use tube no. 80 to pipe six petals from center, with a white frosting. Then, using no. 2 plain tube and red frosting pipe a ring in center completing flower.

At right of fantasy flower is a daffodil. Use light-yellow frosting, with tube no. 81, to make cup. Then, with a deeper shade of yellow frosting, make six petals, starting them narrow, gradually widening, then decreasing to a graceful, tapered point. After piping with tube no. 2 and pale green frosting, complete by adding two or three graceful leaves to stem.

SQUARE TUBES

No. 82. This tube made the two square lines shown; then they were decorated with square beads made with that same tube. They complement the cake when used as a border on the extreme outside edge.

Nos. 83 and 84. Either of these smaller square tubes may be used for the scallops shown; they are finished with a dot between every two scallops.

No. 85. The curved lines and triangular beads shown are made with this tube.

BORDER TUBES

Nos. 86, 87, 88. If you use an up-and-down motion of the hand with any one of these tubes, you will soon be able to duplicate the outstanding borders shown. They are versatile and permit the user to originate his own designs.

In the illustration for tube no. 88, tube no. 2 or 3 makes the tiny circlet between every two scallops.

TRIPLE LINE TUBE

No. 89. This is often called a weaving tube. It is preferred by beginners for basket work, because parallel lines can be made in one operation, as shown.

FRENCH LEAF TUBES

Nos. 94 and 95. These tubes are specially for intricate fern work, borders, and various special leaves. No. 94 is the smaller and is used for even more delicate work.

DROP FLOWER TUBE

No. 96. So easy to use! A slight pressure on the decorating bag makes an individual flower appear. Before releasing it, give one tiny push forward, making a distinct center indentation, which you can fill with contrasting color.

FULL BLOOM ROSE TUBE

No. 97. As a first step, with this tube make a small dome as in fig. 1. Next, with bag in vertical position, make a row of petals snug up against this dome, as in fig. 2 and 3. As you progress with more petals, allow bag to assume a more horizontal position, with rose opening as in full bloom.

SHELL TUBE

No. 98. This interesting little shell tube is wonderful for centers and many other decorations. It produces shell-like designs, individual or joined together in a border.

SPECIAL BORDER AND GARLAND TUBES

No. 99. Three distinct designs may be accomplished with this tube. By holding bag perpendicularly, and with a steady hand, a straight line may be made. By using an up-and-down wavy motion, you will have a wavy border. A side-to-side wavy motion creates a more important looking border for a larger cake.

No. 100. There is a marked similarity between tubes no. 99 and 100. However, being larger, tube no. 100 is especially fine for borders in contrasting colors and for wavy garlands. These may be finished with small circles made with tube No. 2 between every two scallops.

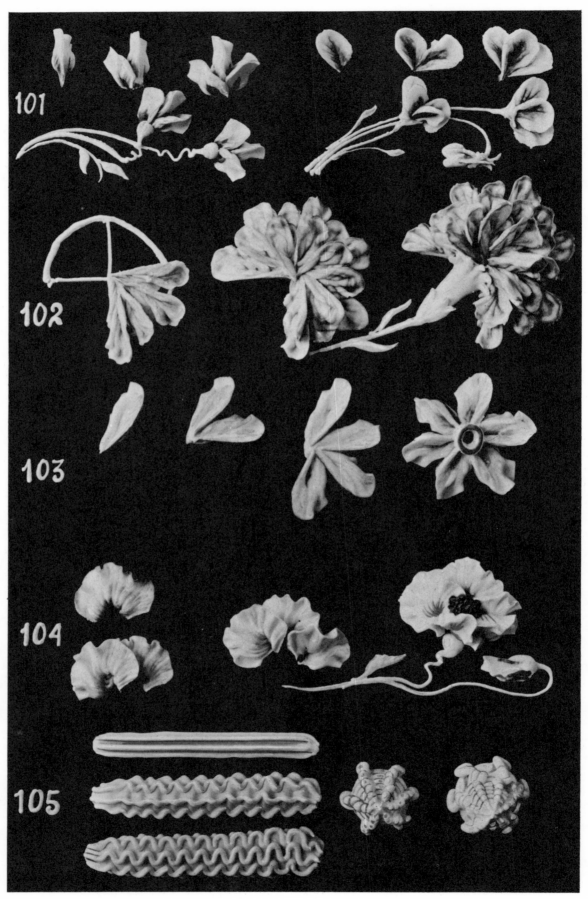

FLOWER TUBES

No. 101. This tube makes pale-pink or white sweet peas or violets, directly on the cake, if desired, as shown.

No. 102. This tube makes a white, pink or red carnation directly on the cake in the steps shown opposite. In starting out, make a cross on the cake slightly smaller than over-all size of carnation. Then draw an incomplete circle, only covering three quarters of the cross as shown. This acts as a guide in piping on the twenty or more uneven flower petals; the fourth quarter is left open for the seed pod.

No. 103. With this tube, six petaled narcissus are quite easy to make in the step-by-step method shown.

No. 104. With this tube you can make orange, salmon, or scarlet poppies right on the cake. Make first petal flat on cake, with slight wavy motion. Make a second petal on left, third on right, each overlapping about half of first petal. The fourth is made directly under the third, by holding tube at an angle. The final petal stands straight up, partly overlapping the fourth. Use tube no. 2 for black icing dots

in center, tube no. 4 and pale-green icing for seed pod. Add stems with darker icing and make scarlet bud with tube no. 102; use tube no. 65 for few green leaves.

OVERPIPING BORDER TUBES

No. 105. The illustration opposite shows three ideal borders. The first was made by holding tube no. 105 at an angle and drawing out in a straight line. The second was made with a slight up-and-down wavy motion. A side-to-side wavy motion was used for the third.

SPECIAL DROP-FLOWER TUBES

Nos. 136, 190, 193, 199, 217 and 224. These tubes make most attractive flowers, including daisies, merely by touching the cake with the tube and twisting it slightly until sufficient frosting has emerged to form a flower. They're quick and easy and give great charm and a professional touch to one's cake.

SPECIAL ROSE TUBES

Nos. 124, 125, 126 and 127. These special large tubes are nice for making large roses and other large-petaled flowers.

TO MAKE PAPER-CONE DECORATOR

From bond or parchment paper, cut 11″ x 8″ x 8″ triangle (or fold square of waxed paper into triangle). Hold in right hand with long side at bottom, thumb at center of long side.

With left hand, bring lower left-hand corner A up to corner B to shape cone. Hold points A and B together with left hand. Bring corner

C around cone so that points A, B, and C meet; fold points down into cone. Cut off about ¾″ of bottom tip. Drop indicated tube into cone.

Half fill decorator with frosting. Fold corners D and E to middle as shown; then fold top down.

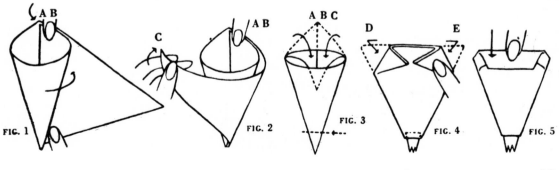

FIG. 1   FIG. 2   FIG. 3   FIG. 4   FIG. 5

For the Sweetest Birthday
(pictured on p. 25)

Several days ahead:

Make **2 doz. Susan's two-tone roses and rosebuds**, p. 28; refrigerate. Also, if desired, make and bake **2 heart-shaped cake layers of Orange Heart Cake**, p. 172; or use **favorite cake mix**; then freeze.

Early on the day:

1. On cake plate, fill and frost thawed cake layers with **1 batch Snow Peak, p. 178**, tinted lightly with **drop or two of blue food color.**

2. Mound some frosting on upper left-hand corner of cake top; arrange largest roses on mound; "shower" rest over cake top, down side.

3. Make **½ batch Posie Cream, p. 177**; tint some **blue**, some **green**, a little **yellow**, with **food colors**. For forget-me-nots, use **tube no. 4 in decorating bag**; press out 4 little dots of blue Posie Cream; use yellow for center dot. For leaves, use **leaf tube no. 68** with green Posie Cream; use same cream, with **plain tube for writing no. 4**, to make "16".

4. Cut **16 candles** to go, step-fashion, half way around cake plate; stick to plate with **modeling clay**. Add **smilax sprays**.

Cake of a Lifetime
(pictured on p. 26)

Two days before wedding:

1. Make **Posie Cream, p. 177**; with **yellow food color** tint half of it pale yellow, half deep yellow. As in **Susan's Posies, p. 28**, make **20 small two-tone yellow roses, 10 small pale yellow roses**, then **10 small deep-yellow roses**. Also, make **15 full-blown yellow roses**, adding 4 more overlapping petals, and slanting thin upper part of tube slightly outward. Freeze each rose, with paper backing, as made.

Day before wedding:

1. Generously grease, then flour bottoms of 3-pan tier-cake set (pans measure 13″ by 2½″, 10″ by 2½″, 7″ by 2½″).

2. Start heating oven to 350° F. Make up **1 large pkg. yellow-cake mix**; pour into 13″ pan; refrigerate. Quickly make up **second pkg.**; add to batter in 13″ pan. Bake 70 min., or until cake tester, inserted in center, comes out clean. Cool 10 min.; remove from pan, cool.

3. When 13″ cake is almost done, make up **third pkg. of mix**; pour into 10″ pan; refrigerate. Make up **fourth pkg. of mix**; pour half of batter into 10″ pan, rest into 7″ pan. Place 10″ pan at back of oven, 7″ pan at front; bake 10″ cake 50 to 55 min., 7″ cake 45 min., or till done. Cool as above.

4. Make **batch of Flower Cream**, p. 176.

5. With **foil**, cover a **round wood board, 14″ wide by ¼″ thick**. On it invert 13″ cake; lightly frost top, sides. Set 10″ layer on top; frost. Set 7″ layer on top; frost.

6. Cut slice from bottom of **unfrosted bakers' cupcake** to level it. Set on top tier, 1½″ in from back edge and left side; frost lightly. Cut **another cupcake** into five ¼″ slices. Place one slice at angle, so top rests against top of first cupcake, base on top tier. Repeat with other four slices, all around cupcake, making mound which slants slightly toward cake center; frost with rest of frosting. Let stand out overnight.

Early on the day:

1. Make **second batch of Flower Cream**; refrost cake and board. Set on large tray.

2. Make **third batch of Flower Cream**; with **tube no. 29 in decorating bag**, press out row of rosettes around base of top tier. Repeat around base and top edge of middle tier, and around top edge of bottom tier; make a double row around bottom of cake.

3. Then, with **pick**, trace lines across and down side of cake as guides for placing roses. Then, take **each rose from freezer**; remove paper; spread back with frosting, set in place.

4. Now tuck **real rosebuds** in place. Then, with **green food color**, tint ¾ cup Flower Cream pale green; use with **tube no. 68 in decorating bag** to make a few leaves among roses and buds. With white frosting and **tube no. 29 in decorating bag**, make rosettes between roses, cascading a few down sides. Refrigerate cake till needed.

24

For the Sweetest Birthday

Cake of a Lifetime

There's a wedding in your future, and — we know just how you feel! — every detail of that day of days must be perfect. Including, certainly, a cake that's really made to dream on. This one, with its fabulous cascade of flowers, is just *that* special. Special because it can be made at home. Made-to-order at home, really –– because it was designed to look as beautiful and unique as a Paris bridal veil.

GALA ANNIVERSARY CAKE

Sugared roses bloom on its snowy terraces, and its diamond shape is — as you might guess — a symbolic tribute to a specially remembered day.

Roses

TUBE NO. **127**

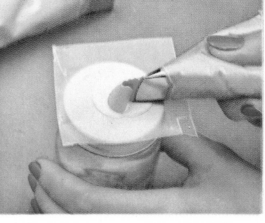

1. For two-tone rose, Susan uses bag of deep-pink Posie Cream. With wide part of tube no. 127 resting on paper-covered jar top, she presses out frosting, slowly turning jar with other hand, until tight budlike center petal is made.

Susan's Posies

For Posie Cream, See p. 177.

For decorating bags and tubes, see p. 11.

Pansies

1. Susan uses bag of yellow and white Posie Cream. Holding bag almost upright, with wide part of tube 123 resting on jar, she presses out first petal near edge of jar top. As she presses, she pivots tube to right, making fan-like petal.

TUBE NO. **123**

TUBE NO. **80**

Chrysanthemums

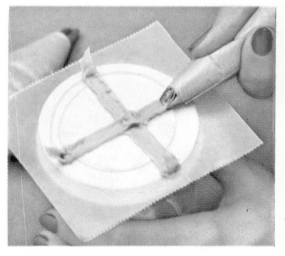

1. Susan first uses bag of light-purple frosting. With rounded side of tube no. 80 resting on jar top, she presses out 4 petals, starting each at center of jar. For stand-up petal ends, she lifts tube from paper, while pressing out frosting.

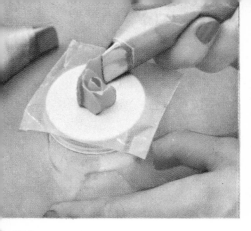

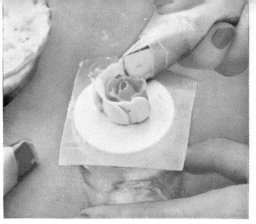

2. Using same bag in same position, while slowly turning jar, Susan presses out small petal, about ½″ long, against center petal of rose. Then she continues around, making 3 or 4 more petals that slightly overlap.

3. Using bag of light-pink frosting, Susan makes about 4 more overlapping petals. She has learned that she gets the best roses by turning jar counterclockwise, rather than moving tube, as she presses out petals.

4. For full-blown effect, Susan presses out 4 more overlapping petals, slanting upper part of tube slightly outward. She firms up rose in ice-cube tray to make it easier to put on cake.

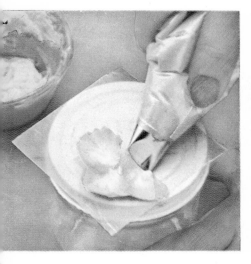

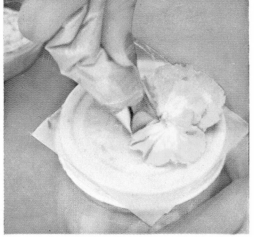

2. Susan makes second petal as in step 1, placing it beside and slightly overlapping first. Then she makes another row of 2 petals, slightly overlapping row above. Next she turns jar so first row of petals is close to her.

3. To press out last petal, she starts with tube pointing toward herself and resting at center of pansy. Slowly turning jar with other hand, she makes large fan-like petal that slightly overlaps third and fourth petals.

4. Now Susan touches up pansies with clean new paintbrush and food colors, blending them for best shade. Then pansies go into ice-cube tray a few minutes before arranging on cake.

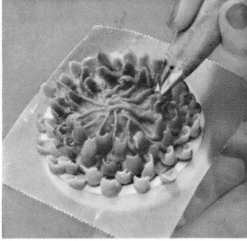

2. Now, starting from center each time, Susan presses out 12 more radiating petals, or enough to cover entire jar top. She doesn't worry if some of stand-up petal ends break off; chrysanthemum looks more lifelike.

3. Next Susan makes another layer of petals, placing them between petals of first layer. Then, switching to bag of dark-purple frosting, she continues piling layers of petals until center of flower is filled.

4. After firming up chrysanthemums in ice-cube tray, as in step 4 of roses, Susan carefully peels off paper. With help of spatula, she groups flowers on mound of frosting on frosted cake.

Camellia Cake

TO CROWN HOLIDAY MENUS

Make this pink-frosted, fruit-and-nut-filled cake with
its wreath of flowers, and you have the extra, gala touch
to make a holiday party really special. If it's to be
an evening of bridge, for instance, you might provide
real camellias from the florist's for the ladies to wear.
Crown it all with the cake and coffee, served in candle
glow from your prettiest china.

COCONUT SWIRL CAKE:
angel cake baked in
an ovenproof bowl, then
frilled and filled with
coconut-cherry frosting and
topped with gumdrop roses

Autumn Festival Cake—
Frosted and Garlanded

Gala Anniversary Cake
(pictured on p. 27)

About one week ahead:

Make and bake **Southern Wedding Cake, p. 173** twice, making four 13″ x 9″ x 2″ cakes; cool, wrap, refrigerate as directed.

The day before the party:

Make and bake **yellow cakes** as follows:

1. Start heating oven to 350° F. Prepare two 10″ x 6″ x 2″ baking pans as cake-mix label directs.

2. Make up **one large pkg. yellow cake mix** as label directs. Divide between the two 10″ x 6″ x 2″ pans. Bake for 20 to 25 min., or until cake tester inserted in center comes out clean; cool. Make up a **second large pkg. yellow cake mix;** bake in two prepared 10″ x 6″ x 2″ pans as before; cool.

3. Prepare a 9″ x 9″ x 2″ pan. Make up, bake, cool a **third large pkg. yellow cake mix** in this, as label directs.

Meanwhile, make roses, ferns, frosting:

SPARKLING SUGARED ROSES AND FERNS

9 pale-pink roses	2 egg whites
7 white roses	2 teasp. water
Very fine granulated sugar	8 fern sprays

1. Separate petals of two roses, one white, one pink; reserve medium and small petals; discard large outer petals. Lightly cover bottom of **about four large shallow pans or trays** with sugar.

2. With **fork,** slightly beat egg whites with water. Carefully dip petals, one by one, in this egg mixture. Drain well; remove excess with **tiny paint-brush;** now sprinkle on both sides with sugar; lay in pan of sugar. Repeat until all rose petals have been sugared, etc.; dry overnight.

3. Now lightly brush egg whites left from roses over top of one fern spray; sprinkle with sugar; lay in pan of sugar; repeat with seven more sprays; dry overnight.

4. Make **two separate batches of Snow White Frosting, p. 178.** Cover each with **foil.**

Early on the day:

Shape diamond cake:

1. Cover **diamond-shaped board, ¼″ thick, 20¼″ long, 12¼″ wide, and 12″ on each side,** with **foil.** Cut each 13″ x 9″ x 2″ fruitcake in half diagonally, making eight triangles in all. On board, gently arrange four of fruitcake triangles to fit diamond shape, trimming as needed. (Cut pieces may be frozen for later use.) Top with four remaining fruit cake triangles; then trim to same size and shape. Thinly fill and frost surfaces, filling in cracks on top and making cake level. This is the bottom tier.

2. Now, on top of bottom tier, measure 2″ in from sides all the way around; mark with toothpicks. Next, cut the four 10″ x 6″ x 2″ yellow cakes in half diagonally, making eight triangles. Arrange four of these triangles within the toothpick markers, cutting to fit and forming diamond. Top with remaining four triangles, cut to same size and shape. Remove picks. Lightly fill and frost.

3. Next, on top of second tier, measure 2″ in from each side, marking with toothpicks. Cut the 9″ x 9″ x 2″ yellow cake in half diagonally, making two triangles. Arrange within toothpick markers, cutting to fit and forming diamond. Remove picks. Lightly frost.

Now Decorate Cake:

1. On **large tray** lay **four 2″ wide waxed-paper strips** to form square; set cake on top; generously refrost, keeping diamond shape.

2. Now, in center of top tier, place a frosting mound 1½″ high and 2″ wide, with rounded edges. Overlap six sugared pink rose petals of same size on frosting mound to resemble full-blown wild rose. Make budlike center with two or three smaller pink petals, anchoring in frosting mound. Then drop bits of frosting off toothpicks to fill in center. Drop **6 to 8 silver dragées** in center.

3. Now surround this center rose with four other roses, two white and two pink, made in same way. Then, on center tier, at opposite pointed ends, group a white and a pink rose.

4. Next, at top center of both sides of bottom tier, make a cluster of two pink and two white roses. Then, on each side, at ends of bottom tier, make a pink rose.

5. Snip leaves of desired size from sugared ferns and tuck around roses.

6. Let cake stand out until ready to serve. Then set in place on party table; remove waxed paper. Arrange about **12 unsugared ferns** around base as pictured.

Camellia Cake

(pictured on p. 30)

Day before:

1. Make **Pink Camellia Cream**, p. 177. Cut **fifteen 3″ waxed-paper squares**. Get out **capped small jar**, 2″ or 3″ across top.

2. Shake **1 or 2 drops red food color** into ½ cup Camellia Cream; with metal spatula, cut through it once or twice for marbleized effect. Use a little, in **decorating bag, with tube no. 125**, to seal first paper square to jar top.

3. Then, hold tube almost horizontally over waxed-paper square, with thin edge near outer edge of jar. Press out cream, gently swinging tube in to within ½″ of imaginary center of camellia, then out, making a slightly ruffled petal 1¼″ long. **Without breaking flow of cream**, raise tube almost vertically over petal just made, and top it with another, not quite overlapping on outer edge.

4. Then, **while still pressing out cream**, bring tube down to a point slightly beyond edge of lower petal; break off.

5. Now, make second petal, snug against first, as in steps 3, 4. Make third petal in same way, except, in step 4, bring tube all around center of camellia, then break off. Now, from end of **toothpick**, drop enough bits of cream to partially fill its center.

6. Then, with same bag and tube, press out tight bud on top of **a food-color bottle**. With picks, carefully slide it to center of camellia. With wide spatula, set camellia, with paper backing, on tray in freezer. Repeat steps 2 through 6, making **13 camellias** in all.

On the day:

1. Make up **2 large pkg. yellow-cake mix**, baking each in greased, floured 9″ x 9″ x 2″ pan at 350° F. 50 min., or till done. Cool in pans on racks 15 min.; remove, cool.

2. Now stack two cakes; then, with sharp knife, cut off four corners, making an eight-sided cake. Then split layers making four.

3. Mix **1½ cups minced pecans; 1½ cups finely crumbled macaroons; 20 maraschino cherries, finely snipped; 3 tablesp. sherry**.

4. Make up **2 pkg. fluffy-white-frosting mix**. To 1½ cups, add pecan mixture. Tint rest pale pink, p. 10.

5. Place **four 3″ waxed-paper strips** in square on round tray. Stack cake layers on it, spreading each with nut mixture. Frost cake lightly with pink frosting. Refrost, making peak with spatula at all eight corners. Press **2 washed, camellia leaves** to base of each side.

At serving time:

Remove paper from each camellia; tuck between leaves. In serving, first remove a camellia and leaves to each dessert plate.

Coconut Swirl Cake

(pictured on p. 31)

Early on the day:

1. In **3-qt. ovenproof mixing bowl**, mix 1 **large pkg. angel-cake mix**. Bake in same bowl at 350° F. 45 min., or till done; cool, inverted on edges of two inverted cake pans.

2. Tint **1⅓ cups coconut pink**, p. 10.

3. On **waxed paper**, well-covered with **granulated sugar**, with a rolling pin, flatten each of **28 red gumdrop strings** into 3½″ by 2¼″ oblong, turning often.

4. Press a **small red gumdrop** onto each of **8 toothpicks**, pinching base against pick. Halve some of oblong gumdrop strings crosswise; wrap one around gumdrop on each pick, so rolled edge becomes petal; press cut edges against pick. If a bud, add 2 or 3 more of these petals. If full-blown rose, keep adding petals, using **whole**, thinly rolled gumdrop strings, wrapped lengthwise, as outer ones. Make 8 **roses** in all.

5. On cake stand, lay 2″ wide waxed-paper strips in square; carefully invert cake on it. With knife, split into three layers.

6. Make **2 pkg. fluffy-white-frosting mix**; to 2½ cups add **1 cup coconut, 1 cup drained, quartered maraschino cherries, 1 cup broken pecans**. Spread between and over layers.

7. Place pick in top center of cake. With **small spatula**, make frosting swirl that starts at base and curves up side of cake, tapering off to point at top. Repeat around cake—we had sixteen. Press **pink coconut** into every other swirl. Remove paper. Set roses on top.

34

Autumn Festival Cake

(pictured on p. 32)

Day before, make marzipan:

In large bowl, knead **1 cup soft canned almond paste, packed,** till pliable. Knead in **2 unbeaten egg whites;** gradually add **6¼ cups sifted confectioners' sugar** or enough to make pliable dough.

Use marzipan to make these fruits:

Apples:

1. Mix **¼ teasp. liquid green food color, 1 teasp. water.** Knead about ⅛ teasp. of this into ¾ cup marzipan to make pale green. On **cornstarch-dusted waxed paper,** form it into 14" roll; cut crosswise into seven 2" pieces.

2. Now roll each marzipan piece into apple shape; stick a **whole clove** into bottom. Leave 3 apples green; brush cheeks of rest with ⅛ **teasp. liquid red food color** mixed with **1 teasp. water.** Dry on tray.

Bananas:

1. Mix **¼ teasp. liquid yellow food color, 1 teasp. water.** Knead ¼ teasp. of this into ½ cup marzipan to make banana color; on **cornstarch-dusted waxed paper,** form it into 12" roll; slice into seven 1¾" pieces.

2. Now shape each marzipan piece into a banana; pinch ends slightly so they taper; slightly flatten top to resemble banana. Next, **make some brown color** as food color label directs; with it and **fine brush,** paint markings on bananas. Dry on tray.

Pears:

1. Mix ⅛ **teasp. liquid yellow food color, 1 teasp. water;** knead ¼ teasp. of this into ½ cup marzipan. On **cornstarch-dusted waxed paper,** form into 12" roll; slice into six 2" pieces.

2. Now roll each marzipan piece into a round ball, then into a cone, bending top slightly. In top of each pear, insert **stick of dried rosemary,** to resemble pear stem. With **3 drops liquid yellow food color,** mixed with **1 teasp. water,** and a fine brush, paint surface of each to resemble ripe pear. Make blush on two of them with red color used for apples. Dry on tray.

Apricots:

1. Mix **3 drops liquid yellow food color, 1 teasp. water.** Knead ½ teasp. of this, **3 drops undiluted liquid yellow food color, 2 drops liquid red food color** into ½ cup marzipan to make apricot color. On **cornstarch-dusted waxed paper,** form into 12" roll; slice into eight 1½" pieces. Roll each into ball; with **wooden skewer,** make crease down one side to resemble apricot. Dry on tray.

Cherries:

1. Mix **¼ teasp. liquid blue food color** with **1 teasp. water;** knead about ⅛ teasp. of this into ½ cup marzipan to tint light blue. Add ¾ **teasp. undiluted liquid red food color** to make cherry color. On **cornstarch-dusted waxed paper,** form into a 17" roll; slice into thirty-four ½" pieces.

2. Now roll each marzipan piece into a small cherry, and set on tray. Then heat **1 tablesp. white corn syrup** with **1 teasp. water;** use to brush each cherry; let dry.

Early on the day:

1. **Make cake:**

Make and bake **1 large pkg. each of chocolate (or fudge) cake mix, yellow (or white) cake mix, and spicecake mix** in six 9" layer cake pans as label directs; cool.

2. **Make Harvest Filling:**

Simmer **2 cups dark raisins** in **1½ cups water,** uncovered, until soft; stir in **1 tablesp. cornstarch** mixed with **1 tablesp. cold water,** ½ **teasp. vanilla;** cool.

3. **Make Pastel Frosting:**

Make up **2 pkg. fluffy-white frosting mix** as label directs. Add **few drops liquid green food color** to tint pale green.

4. **Assemble cake:**

On cake plate lay **4 strips waxed paper, 2" wide,** in square. On it place 1 chocolate layer; spread with half of Harvest Filling; top with 1 yellow layer; spread with rest of filling; top with spicecake layer. (Freeze extra layers to use later).

Lightly frost cake with Pastel Frosting to set crumbs; swirl rest of frosting on side and top. Pull out paper strips. Garnish cake with marzipan fruits, **tiny green leaves.**

In serving, remove one fruit to each dessert plate; cut cake wedge, set nearby.

Sugarplum Tree

(pictured on p. 41)

2 tablesp. molasses
2 tablesp. flour
China dog and cat
2 tablesp. semisweet
    chocolate pieces
3 9" cake layers
Snow Peak, p. 178

12" tree branch
Foil or saran
Candies: lollipops,
    candy canes, choco-
    late kisses, candy pin
    wheels, marshmallow
    bits, round and long
    gumdrops.

1. **Day before**: Mix molasses with flour; use, with **child's paintbrush**, to "paint" dog. Over hot, **not boiling**, water melt chocolate; use to "paint" cat. Also, make, bake, cool, cake layers and fill with Snow Peak; set on cake stand; frost; refrigerate.

2. **On party day**: Cut blooming branch from tree; snip off some twigs, leaves; wrap bottom in foil; insert in center of cake.

3. Unwrap lollipops; with **putty**, press to edge of cake plate. Or if you prefer, cut lollipop sticks short; then press lollipops into frosting around side of cake.

4. On tree, hang candy canes; to branches, attach candies with **confectioners' sugar** mixed with **bit of water** to form paste. Sprinkle a few gumdrops around cake stand. Set dog on cake, cat in tree.

Jaunty Jack-in-a-Box

(pictured on p. 41)

2 favorite 8" cake
    layers
Snow Peak, p. 178
Heavy cardboard
Foil
1 6-oz. pkg. semisweet
    chocolate pieces

Food colors
1 unfrosted cupcake
Lollipop stick
Long and tiny round
    gumdrops
Toasted flaked coconut
Heavy paper for hat

1. From cake layers, cut two 4" squares. Make Snow Peak; use some to fill squares, making "box". From cardboard, cut two 4" squares; cover one with foil; with bit of frosting, "glue" bottom of box to it. Over **hot, not boiling**, water, melt chocolate; use to frost top of box and one side of remaining cardboard square (lid). Let lid set out to cool.

2. Tint 1 cup frosting pink; ½ cup yellow; ½ cup green. With white frosting, frost sides of box, saving enough for lid.

3. With pink frosting and spatula, make diagonal stripes on box (save some for lid).

4. With yellow frosting, frost cupcake all over. In center top of box, insert lollipop stick; on it, secure cupcake on side. Make face on cupcake, using sliced round black gumdrops for eyes, halved long red gumdrop for mouth. For hair, sprinkle cupcake with toasted coconut. From 5" square of heavy paper, make conical hat; trim base in straight line; frost green; set in place.

5. Frost other side of lid with white frosting, adding pink stripes. Lean lid against Jack, as shown, with chocolate side down. Prop lid at back with toothpicks.

The Red-Barn Cake

(pictured on p. 43)

Day before:

1. Make up **one large pkg. yellow cake mix** as label directs; turn into greased, floured 10″ x 6″ x 2″ loaf pan; bake at 350° F. 50 min.; cool in pan; remove. Repeat with **two more large packages of same mix.**

2. Make, bake **fourth large pkg. yellow-cake mix** in two greased, floured 46-oz. fruit-juice cans at 350° F. 35 to 40 min.; cool in cans; remove. Wrap, store all cakes.

3. Prepare **Ornamental Frosting,** p. 177; **Red Butter Cream Frosting,** p. 178; store as directed. Tint **2⅔ cups flaked coconut** delicately with **green food color,** p. 10.

Early on the day:

1. **Make silo:** Cut rounded top from one cylinder cake. Lightly frost 5″ by 5″ piece of cardboard with Ornamental Frosting; on it, set cake, cut side up. Frost cut side; top with second cylinder cake.

2. **Make barn:** Cut rounded top from two of loaf cakes. Spread a 10″ by 6″ rectangle of Ornamental Frosting on a 12″ by 8″ piece of cardboard; on it, place one loaf cake, cut side up. Frost cut side; top with second loaf cake, cut side up. Frost cut side; top with third loaf cake, rounded side up. Let frosting set a bit. Mark lengthwise line down center of top cake; with sharp knife, trim to resemble two slanting sides of roof. Even off sides of barn proper.

3. With Red Butter-Cream Frosting, lightly frost sides of barn, silo; dry. Frost again; then, with small spatula, make rows of horizontal ridges to resemble shingles.

4. **Make barn roof:** Cut 10″ by 8″ rectangle from light cardboard; make a lengthwise cut down center to form two sides of roof. Lightly frost cake roof with Ornamental Frosting; press cardboard roof in place.

5. **Make silo roof:** Mark center of a 5″ circle of light cardboard. Make a slash to center; overlap cut edges ¾″ to form cone-shape roof. Frost on inside with Ornamental Frosting; press lightly on top of silo; dry.

6. **For cupola on center top of barn:** Cut 1½″ by 6″ rectangle from cardboard; starting at 1½″ side, fold into fourths; unfold. From base of first and third squares, cut small triangle. Tape edges, forming cupola.

7. **For cupola roof:** Cut 3¾″ cardboard circle; fold in half; starting at center, fold ends in to make six equal sections when unfolded. Cut two adjacent sections out of circle; cut straight across bottom of remaining sections; join two sides with tape.

8. Frost cupola with Red Butter-Cream. Using Ornamental Frosting in **decorating bag with tube no. 48,** and starting at outer edge of pointed silo roof, make overlapping rows of shingles around roof. Next, starting at lengthwise edge of one side of barn roof, make similar shingles; repeat on other side. Make line of frosting along top edge of roof as ridgepole.

9. **Press cupola onto center top of barn roof;** attach its roof with frosting; cover with shingles as above. Make tiny paper weathercock; attach with pick to cupola roof.

10. Last, on barn, with Ornamental Frosting **in decorating bag and tube no. 8,** make four doors and four circles decorated with **gumdrop** or tinted frosting design, known as hex sign. Sprinkle green-tinted flaked coconut around base of barn and silo as grass.

Bobby's Balloon Cake

(pictured on p. 42)

Day before:

Make, bake, cool **one 10″ angel or chiffon cake.** Then remove from pan to rack. Store.

On party day:

1. Set cake on cake plate. Use **Snow Peak,** **p. 178,** to frost top, sides.

2. Cut **large green, red, and yellow gumdrops** cross-wise into thin slices. Arrange, cut side up, here and there, on sides and top of cake to resemble balloons.

3. Attach a string to each, painted in with toothpick dipped in **food color.** Add **green and yellow candles.**

Jelly-Roll Milk Truck

(pictured on p. 44)

Cardboard; foil
1 8-oz. baker's pound
   cake
½ batch Snow Peak
   p. 178
2 5" by 3" bakers'
   jelly rolls
1 batch Snow Cream,
   p. 178
Decorating tube no. 3
Decorating bags
2 long black, 2 yellow

gumdrops
2 foil-covered candies
3 licorice pastels
1 foil-covered 2½"
   jar cap
2 pipe cleaners
6 round peppermint
   candies
2 tablesp. cocoa
Dark-brown sugar
Bottled green sugar
Plastic animals, fence

Early on day:

1. From cardboard, cut piece 13" by 4"; cover with foil. From end of pound cake, cut slice 1" thick; from this cut off crosswise strip 1" wide; lay across cardboard, 2" from front end; lay remaining strip 5" behind.

2. From end of pound cake, cut slice 2½" thick; out of this, cut block of cake 1¼" by 1¼", leaving L-shaped piece. Trim ½" off top of cab, top corners of motor. Frost with Snow Peak. With blend of red, blue, yellow, green food colors, tint a little Snow Peak gray; use to make side windows, windshield.

3. From pound cake, cut 1" square; place on cardboard between cake strips to support truck body. Cut 13" by 2½" piece of cardboard; cover with foil; set on cake strips.

4. Place jelly rolls end to end; on two long sides, 1½" up from base, cut out lengthwise wedge ½" deep, 1" high. Set rolls at back end of cardboard. On top set 2½" by ½" cake round. Frost all with Snow Peak.

5. Tint half of Snow Cream green; use with **tube no. 3** in **decorating bag** to outline ends, sides, top of truck body, doors, windows of cab, and to make radiator grill, cap. Set cab in place at front of cardboard.

6. Into frosting on cab, press black gumdrop on either side for fender; for bumper, use 2 yellow ones; for headlights, foil-covered candies; for license plate and brake lights on back of truck, licorice pastels.

7. Top truck with jar top. For ladder on sides, halve each pipe cleaner; cover with foil; tape steps, made of foil strips, to sides.

8. For wheels, with frosting, "glue" peppermint candies to crosswise cake strips on bottom. To rest of Snow Cream add cocoa; thin, so its spreads, with a little milk. Place in **paper cone;** from tip of cone, cut off ¼". Press out tire around each wheel.

9. For rural setting, arrange truck on table; make road of brown sugar (also cover cardboard under truck), grass of green sugar. Set animals and fence in place.

Golden Hen

(pictured on p. 44)

Day before:

Dye **12 hard cooked** eggs as egg-dye label directs. Make **2 batches Snow Cream, p. 178;** with **food colors,** tint small amounts green, pink, yellow, etc. Use with **tubes no. 3 and 27,** in **decorating bags,** to trim eggs. Mix **1 can shredded** and **1 can flaked coconut;** toast as on p. 10. Make **two 8" cake layers.**

Early on party day:

1. Make **Snow Peak, p. 178.** Tint ¼ cup pinkish red; tint rest yellow.

2. Halve each cake layer; stack 3 halves, using yellow frosting as "glue." Stand, on cut sides, on foil-covered cardboard oval, 9" by 6". Trim two outside layers so they're shape of hen's body.

3. For tail, from fourth cake half, cut 3" wedge; with **wooden skewers,** attach near end of center layer at slight angle. For head, from cake half, cut shape shown. Have back of head 4½" long, head 2½" wide; round off lower part to fit curve of hen's body. Skewer to front end of center cake layer.

4. Frost hen yellow; then, with **spatula,** make ridges along sides for wings. With pinkish-red frosting, make comb, pulling up frosting with tip of spatula. Split **1 long black gumdrop** lengthwise almost to end; open; secure in place as bill, with **picks.** From **another gumdrop,** cut 2 crosswise slices; use as eyes. Set hen in place on table; surround with nest of toasted coconut, then with eggs.

Old-Woman-in-a-Shoe Cake

(pictured on p. 45)

2 large pkg. yellow
  cake mix
Party Cream, p. 177
1 pkg. fluffy white
  frosting mix
Red food color
Licorice candy
Red cinnamon candies

2 or more pkg. thin 1"
  candy wafers
2 tablesp. cocoa
Short taper candles
Narrow blue ribbon
Round white board or
  cardboard; foil
Tiny rubber children

The Cake Foundation:

Early, day before, make, bake, cool, store cakes, covered. Or bake several days or weeks ahead, then freezer-wrap and freeze. To make cakes, proceed as follows:

1. Start heating oven to 350° F. Grease **well** 10" x 5" x 3" loaf pan.

2. Prepare 1 pkg. cake mix as label directs; turn into loaf pan. Bake about 55 min., or until cake tester inserted in center comes out clean.

3. Cool cake in pan on rack 10 min.; remove from pan; cool on rack. Then store or freeze as preferred.

4. Make and bake second cake in same well-greased 10" x 5" x 3" loaf pan for 55 min., or until done; cool, store, as in step 3.

Shaping the Shoe Cake:

The evening before the party, put the cake together and decorate as directed below. Then refrigerate or freeze it until time to put on the table.

1. Cut a piece of heavy cardboard into an 8½" by 4½" rectangle; round off all four corners with scissors; then cover the cardboard with foil.

2. From the end of one of yellow loaf cakes cut off a 6" piece; set aside both pieces.

3. From other yellow loaf cake, cut off both ends so remaining loaf measures 7".

4. For **toe part of shoe cake:** With small mound of Party Cream, glue the 6" piece of yellow cake to one end of the cardboard so that its cut side is facing in.

5. For **leg part of shoe cake:** Glue the 7" piece of yellow cake, standing up, to other end of cardboard, with its rounded side facing out, and snug against cut side of first piece of cake.

6. Now, with **a sharp paring knife,** carefully round off and trim all corners and edges of cake to resemble shoe.

7. To prepare for peaked roof on the shoe cake: On each side of 7" leg, 1" down from top, make an upward cut to center top of cake; remove these two pieces of cake and reserve them.

8. **For peaked roof:** From the reserved pieces of cake, cut two ½"-thick slices; trim each slice to 3½" by 3¼". Then glue each slice to one slant of leg, so they meet in center, holding them in place with picks.

Frosting Shoe Cake:

1. Now make up the package of frosting mix as label directs; tint it a delicate pink with red food color. Then spread some of it thinly over the entire shoe to set crumbs.

2. Now generously frost shoe with rest of pink frosting, building up shape of shoe over instep and at toe.

3. Next, cut 9 strips of licorice, each 1½" by ¼"; use to make lacings for shoe. Use red cinnamon candies for holes. Cut 2 strips of licorice, each 3" by ¼", for ends of shoelaces. Press in place.

4. **To make the shingles on the roof:** Starting at bottom of roof on each side, overlap thin candy wafers in even, overlapping rows, alternating colors as shown.

5. Into about ½ cup Party Cream, stir the cocoa until smooth and blended. Then use in **decorating bag** with **ribbon tube no. 47** to make the door, shutters, and the sole around the shoe, as shown.

6. Next, using white Party Cream in a **decorating bag,** with **rosette tube no. 28,** outline door and windows on shoe as shown. Complete it with windowpanes, doorknob.

7. Lastly, arrange a row of candles on the ridge of the roof, as shown.

The Yard for the Shoe Cake:

1. Set finished shoe cake on a round, white board or cardboard, with ribbon around edge.

2. Then place some tiny rubber children here and there at play in the yard.

3. In cutting cake, first slice toe part into 6 to 8 slices. Then cut off rest of cake just below roof, being careful of picks. Slice this part of cake into 6 to 8 slices. Or use the shoe as a centerpiece and pass tiny shoe cakes. Makes 12 to 16 servings.

39

Carrousel Cake

(pictured on p. 46)

A week or so ahead, use items below to make two of each animal as directed:

6 large round gumdrops
30 small round gumdrops
10 candied fruit slices
4 white Life Savers
4 candy peanuts
Colored toothpicks
1 small tube green decorating gel
2 large pkg. yellow-cake mix
2 13" paper doilies, with 2" lacy edges
Double-faced cellophane tape

1 13" circle heavy white paper
1 pkg. plastic decorating tips, p. 11
1 6-oz. tube prepared pink icing, p. 11
1 large green gumdrop
1 6-oz. tube prepared green icing, p. 11
1 13" cardboard circle
Foil; toothpicks
1 pkg. fluffy white-frosting mix
24 striped straws
24 gumdrop strings*

---

* Let stand out several days to harden.

Giraffe

Body: Place 2 large gumdrops, flat sides together; fasten with pick; snip off pick's end.

Neck, Head: String 3 small gumdrops, through centers, on pick, leaving ½" of pick at one end, ¼" at other. From curved side of a fruit slice, cut wedge 1" by ½"; fasten to ¼" end of pick; insert ½" end of pick in center top of body.

Four Legs: Push ends of 4 picks into centers of 4 small gumdrops; push other ends, at slight angle, into body.

Tail: From fruit slice used for neck, cut piece ½" long; snip to resemble tail. Push a pick, 1" long, partway into tail, other end into center of rear body gumdrop. Adjust giraffe's feet, head so he stands well.

Bird

Two Legs: Cut 2 picks 1¾" long; insert each in round side of large gumdrop.

Body: Into center of curved side of a fruit slice, push ends of two legs.

Head, Beak: From curved side of another fruit slice cut wedge ½" long; press into beak shape; push 1" piece of pick partway into its broader end. Press a Life Saver into each side of beak. With exposed pick end, fasten head and beak to body, ¼" from top of fruit slice.

Horse

Body: Use 1 candy peanut.

Four Legs, Feet: Push 4 picks into 4 small gumdrops; push them, at slight angle, into bottom of peanut body so it stands erect.

Head: From curved side of fruit slice, cut piece 1½" by 1"; use its curved side as back of head; snip ¼" by ¼" piece out of base as nose; make upward slit as nostrils. Insert pick part way into base, other end into end of peanut.

Tail: Make, fasten as in Giraffe above.

Zebra

Make like Horse, but use tube of green decorating gel for body stripes; let dry. Use same gel to make eyes on all animals.

Early on the day, make and decorate cake:

1. Make up 2 pkg. cake mix, one after other, as directed; pour into greased, floured, round cake pan 13" in diameter, 2½" deep. Bake at 350° F., 60 min., or until done. Cool in pan 15 min., then remove cake from pan to rack.

2. Cut lacy edges from doilies; in edges make ⅛" pleats, 2" apart. With cellophane tape fasten, end to end, around edge of 13" paper circle. Lay this canopy on cookie sheet. With plastic star tip screwed onto pink icing tube, make rosettes every 2" around canopy; make one on large green gumdrop; dry.

3. Screw star tip on green icing tube; make green rosette between every two pink ones. With writing tip screwed onto pink icing tube, outline edge of canopy. Dry.

4. Cover 13" cardboard circle with foil. On it set cake; frost cake with frosting mix.

5. To top of each of 16 striped straws (poles) fasten ½" piece cellophane tape. Press 8 against frosting at equal intervals around cake. Between these, 3" in from top cake edge, push 8 more into cake. With tape, secure 8 more together as one pole; to top press 1" piece of tape; insert in center of cake.

6. Between each pair of outside poles press 3 gumdrop strings into frosting, at slight angle. On top of cake, between each pair of outside poles, set an animal. Center canopy on top of poles, pressing so tape holds; top with the frosted gumdrop. Serve an animal with each wedge of cake.

40

Sugarplum Tree

Jaunty Jack-in-a-Box

Bobby's Balloon Cake

Red Barn Cake

Jelly Roll Milk Truck

Golden Hen

Old-Woman-in-a-Shoe Cake

Carrousel Cake

Raggedy Annabel

(pictured opposite)

Day before:

1. Bend **piece of cardboard, 24" by 8",** in half crosswise; set, at angle, on table, against firm support. Cut off 2" wedge from end of **a large jelly roll (5" by 3");** set roll on cut end against upright part of cardboard. Top with **3" piece from a second large jelly roll;** round off top for head.

2. Unroll **third large jelly roll;** cut in half crosswise; reroll each piece; place on lower part of cardboard as sides of skirt. Fill in center with pieces left from large jelly rolls, cutting to fit as necessary.

3. For legs and arms, arrange **4 small jelly rolls** (2½" by 1"), as shown; round off ends of legs. Now on **cardboard,** with pencil, trace

around doll; remove cake pieces; cut cardboard into doll shape; cover with **foil**; replace cake pieces.

4. Make **Snow Peak, p. 178.** To ½ cup Snow Peak add 1 drop each **red** and **yellow food color** to make flesh color; spread on doll as face, knees, hands. Spread on ½ cup white Snow Peak as apron. Tint 1 cup Snow Peak **yellow**; tint rest **pink** and use for doll's dress. With yellow frosting, frost top and sides of head, pulling frosting up with spatula for curls.

5. Make **2 batches Snow Cream, p. 178.**

For socks, use half of Snow Cream, building frosting up to a point at top of doll's foot. Tint rest of Snow Cream **blue**; use with **tube no. 68** in **decorating bag** to make belt and ruffle around apron; with **tube no. 3,** make polka dots on apron, eyes, and trim on socks. Add **half a candied cherry** as mouth; use **melted chocolate** for eyelashes and nose.

On party day:

Carefully, so as not to disturb frosting, set Raggedy Annabel in place on table.

Santa Jigsaw
Jumbo the Clown
Lucinda's House

Santa Jigsaw

(pictured on p. 48)

Early in day:

1. Prepare **1 package yellow-cake mix for two-layer cake** as label directs for 13″ by 9″ baking pan but add ½ **cup raisins.** Bake; cool. Meanwhile, draw a jig-saw face pattern on paper and cut into sections.
2. Place cake on platter, bottom up.
3. Prepare ½ **recipe Ornamental Frosting** p. 177). In paper cone, place ½ cup.
4. Spread thin layer of frosting over cake.

Lay patterns on frosting; with toothpick, outline sections; remove patterns. Pipe frosting around all edges of each section; let dry a few minutes.

5. Meanwhile, add **a few teaspoons water** to frosting in bowl to make a glaze consistency; spoon into white jig-saw spaces. Tint remaining frosting pink with **red food color;** spoon into pink spaces. Tint remaining pink frosting red; spoon into red spaces. Let dry. Pipe eyes, eyebrows and mouth.

Jumbo the Clown

(pictured on p. 48)

Early in day:

1. Prepare **1 package orange cake mix for two-layer cake** as label directs for two 9-inch round cake pans; cool.
2. Prepare **1 package fluffy white frosting mix** as label directs; tint orange with **red and yellow food colors;** reserve ⅓ cup. With remaining, fill and frost cake.
3. Cut about 1 inch from wide end of **1 ice-**

cream cone to make clown's collar; reserve rest of cone. With **orange ribbon,** tie a bow around collar; center collar on cake.

4. With **felt-tip pens,** draw clown face on **ping-pong ball;** with frosting, fasten to collar.
5. For hat, frost reserved cone with frosting. Sprinkle hat with **red-colored sugar;** attach to ball with frosting. Sprinkle sugar around collar to make ruff.

Lucinda's House

(pictured on p. 48)

Early in day:

1. Prepare **two packages poundcake mix,** one at a time, as labels direct; cool. Cover **16″ by 11″ cardboard** with **foil.**
2. Trim rounded top from one cake; place cake, cut side up, on cardboard. For sloping roof, from one cake, from center, cut wedges to each narrow end; from a wedge, cut a 2″ by 2¼″ door.
3. Prepare **2 packages fluffy white frosting mix,** at one time, as labels direct. Melt ½ **square unsweetened chocolate;** stir in ¼ cup frosting; place in paper cone. With **green food color,** tint ½ cup frosting.
4. With some of remaining white frosting, frost top of trimmed cake; set second cake, cut side up, on top; frost top and sides.
5. With frosting, fasten about **20 oblong tea**

cookies in place as roof "tiles."

6. With chocolate frosting, pipe "windows."
7. Separate **2 sugar wafers;** cut pieces into ¾″ squares. With white frosting, attach squares as shutters; attach door and **1 oval cookie window;** with frosting, make doorknob. Cut remaining squares into triangles; with frosting, attach under roof to make eaves.
8. Build chimney up one side of house with **8 nougat candies** and frosting; before adding top piece, make 2 holes in it and insert **2 candy cigarettes;** top with bit of frosting and **piece of cotton** for "smoke."
9. Use remaining white frosting to cover cardboard and part of roof with "snow."
10. With green frosting, frost **2 ice cream cones** for trees; with **one 6-ounce package semi-sweet-chocolate pieces,** make path.

Horseshoe Cake

(pictured on p. 57)

The Cake Foundation:

Bake cakes a day or so ahead; store, covered. Or bake cakes several days or weeks ahead; freezer-wrap; freeze. To make and bake them, proceed as follows:

1. Prepare and bake **1 large pkg. favorite cake mix** as label directs, making two 9″ layers. Cool as directed.

2. Start heating oven to 350° F. Grease well a 10″ x 6″ x 2″ oblong pan. Prepare **second large package of cake mix** as label directs; turn into oblong pan; bake about 35 min., or until cake tester inserted in center comes out clean. Cool as directed.

Shaping and Decorating the Horseshoe:

The evening before the party, put Horseshoe Cake together, decorate, then refrigerate overnight as follows:

1. From center of one 9″ layer, cut, remove, reserve 3″ circle; then cut layer crosswise in half. Place one half on other with some **Range Frosting, p. 178,** as filling. (Save second layer for later dessert.)

2. Place **14″ by 12″ oblong wooden board** or **foil-covered cardboard** so short end faces you. On board, set filled layer, with rounded side at end of board away from you. Set oblong cake on board, with long side against cut sides of layer; "glue" with frosting.

3. Starting at ends of inner arc of layer, with knife, cut down through oblong cake to form horseshoe shape. Remove center piece of cake from oblong (save for a later dessert).

4. Now, where inner arc of layer joins oblong cake, whittle off some cake to widen arc. Also whittle cake into horseshoe shape, 2″ up from both ends.

5. Cut reserved 3″ circle of layer cake in half vertically. Set one half on top of the other, with frosting as filling; halve vertically. With frosting, glue a straight cut side of each half to outside of each end of horseshoe, forming straight line at bottom.

6. Using Range Frosting, generously frost sides, then top, of cake, keeping horseshoe shape. Refrigerate.

7. To serve, set **cowboy, Indian figures,** and **birthday candles,** as shown.

Party Dress

(pictured on p. 58)

4 layers Budget Gold Cake, p. 170; or 4 6″ or 8″ cake layers Snow Peak, p. 178 7″ doll	Foil or saran Food colors Posie Cream, p. 177 Leaf tube, no. 68 Decorating bags Rosette tube, no. 28

The Cake Skirt:

Place bottom cake layer on **circle of cardboard,** cut to fit, or on **cake plate.** Trim next layer a wee bit smaller. Trim third layer a bit smaller than second. Trim fourth layer smaller than third. Out of top 2 layers, cut hole large and deep enough for doll to stand in waist-deep. With a little Snow Peak, "glue" 4 layers together. Wrap doll to waistline in foil or saran; set in hole.

Frosting and Decorating:

Tint Snow Peak delicate blue; use to frost entire cake. On top layer, pile frosting right up to doll's waist. Now pull flat side of spatula up sides of frosted cake, all the way around, to give effect of full skirt. For white "lace" insert, with toothpick outline triangle on front of skirt, making it widest at bottom. Using white Posie Cream and **leaf tube no. 68** in **decorating bag,** start at bottom of triangle to press out overlapping lines of frosting from left to right, in a forward-and-backward motion; fill up triangle.

Using same leaf tube, with half of remaining Posie Cream tinted light blue, make flounces around top of skirt, and blue ruffle around bottom. For bouquet, tint remaining Posie Cream pink, yellow, and green. With **rosette tube no. 28** in **decorating bag,** pile on pink and yellow flowers. With leaf tube, add few green leaves. Insert **candle.**

P.S. We made cupcakes for each little miss to eat.

50

Cinderella Goes to the Ball

(pictured on p. 60)

Any one of these cakes makes an exciting centerpiece, too!

PRINCE CHARMING'S CASTLE

Week or so ahead:

Make **6 turret frames** as in step 1 on p. 60. Make, bake, **1 large pkg. angel food mix** in 10″ tube pan, as directed; cool; freezer-wrap; freeze. Buy **5 knights on horses.**

Two days before party:

Make **Butter Cream, p. 175;** set aside ¾ cup. Use rest to "glue" inverted angel food to **10″ cardboard circle** and to frost it and turrets. **Complete castle** as in steps 1 through 3, p. 60. Set castle on **inverted sea green cake plate** on table, with knights around it. **Two thirds of a chocolate bar** is drawbridge.

FAIRY GODMOTHER AND CINDERELLA

1 large pkg. angel food mix	Snow Peak, p. 178
Two 4″ dolls	One 4″, one 7″ card-board circle
White and pink net	Silver dragées
Foil	Food colors
3 silver and 1 white paper doilies	⅓ cup Butter Cream left from castle
Toothpicks, silver star	

Week or so ahead:

1. Make up angel food mix; use to fill **8 ungreased, individual angel food pans, 3½″ by 1½″,** to within ½″ of tops. Bake at 375° F. 15 to 17 min.; cool 5 min.; remove from pans; cool. (Bake rest of batter for later use.) Freezer-wrap cakes; freeze. For pans see p. 181.

2. Wrap dolls in net strips down to waistline—white for Fairy Godmother, pink for Cinderella. Wrap from waistline down in foil.

Two days before party:

1. Enlarge one side of center hole of each of **5 inverted angel cakes** enough to insert doll. Halve one of 5 cakes crosswise. Stack 2 whole cakes and one of halves for Cinderella; repeat for Fairy Godmother.

2. Trim sides of two top cakes on each, to line up with bottom cake. Insert doll in each.

3. **For Fairy Godmother,** p. 61: Cut **crown** from silver doily, **wings** from 2 silver doilies, glued together. For **wand,** cover toothpick with foil; attach silver star.

Use Snow Peak to glue one doll cake to **4″ cardboard circle;** frost cake lightly; frost again half way up front, pulling frosting up with tip of spatula to make up-and-down folds in **skirt.**

For each scallop in front, pile some frosting on cake's top edge; swirl down to meet folds, then up to waistline.

4. For **train,** pile frosting at back of cake's top; sweep down to bottom. With **dragées** outline scallops, train. Attach wings and floating net to frosting at center back. Tape wand to hand. Adjust crown. Refrigerate.

5. **For Cinderella,** p. 61: For **headband,** cut scalloped strip from white doily; join ends. Tint rest of Snow Peak pale pink; use to glue second doll cake to 7″ cardboard circle, so front of skirt is 1″ in from edge. Frost cake lightly. Now pile frosting on cardboard all around; with flat side of spatula, pull frosting up side of cake to make full skirt. With tip of spatula, pull it up in front for ripples. Make train as in step 4 above.

With toothpick, outline base of overskirt. Tint some Butter Cream deep pink; use with **tube no. 27** in **decorating bag** for rosettes around doll's waist, base of overskirt. Fill in overskirt with rosettes. Make some on headband; set in place. Add 2 roses to bodice, 2 rows of ruching around hemline. Refrigerate.

PUMPKIN COACH

Week or so ahead:

1. Make **coach wheels** as in step 3, p. 61.

2. Trim six **4″-high black horses** with **blankets of red cloth.** Add **gold paper rickrack, trim, rickrack reins, gold paper collar, plumes.**

3. Make, bake, cool **Pumpkin Coach Cake,** p. 173. Trim to pumpkin shape as in step 1, p. 61. Freezer-wrap, freeze.

On party day:

1. Set Pumpkin Coach Cake on plate to fit. Make **Snow Peak, p. 178.** Tint one fourth green. Tint rest orange, p. 10; use to frost cake, making ridges, etc., as in step 2, p. 61.

2. Cut **3″ piece from stem end of banana;** frost green; adjust as pumpkin stem; add **leaves.** Add door cut from **gold paper doily.**

3. Set coach on inverted bonbon dish; prop coach wheels in place. Harness horses to coach with gold paper rickrack.

Note: To complete Cinderella as on p. 61, for background, use **long piece of blue paper** extending over table and up wall. On it, with **chalk,** draw **moon, stars, moat. Chair, slipper, stool,** and **tree** lend atmosphere.

The Cake Clown

For a circus party that couldn't be easier, serve our Cake Clown and pink lemonade.

Day before:

1. Bake **1 large pkg. yellow cake mix** in 13″ x 9″ x 2″ pan. Cool; wrap; store.

2. Cut **13″ by 7″ piece of paper;** fold in half lengthwise; 1½″ down from top of fold, mark hatbrim; 3″ from top, neckline; 6½″ from top, waistline; 10″, crotch.

3. Mark width of waistline, 2½″ from fold; widest part of head, 1¼″ from fold; widest part of pantaloons, 3½″ from fold; toe, 3½″ from fold; heel, 1″ from fold.

4. With marks and drawing as guides, outline one side of clown. Cut out, unfold, and use to cut out **cardboard clown;** cover with **foil.** Make **Clown Cream,** p. 176.

On the day:

1. Lay cardboard clown on cake; with **knife** cut out cake clown. Set on cardboard clown.

2. Make up **1 pkg. fluffy white frosting mix.** Lightly frost cake; frost again.

3. For dots, arrange **large and small, vari-colored gumdrop slices,** cut side up.

4. For shoes, use **2 pieces licorice, 2½″ by ½″,** tapered at one end.

5. For sleeves, tint two thirds of Clown Cream pale yellow with **yellow food color;** use in **decorating bag,** with **tube no. 115.**

6. For ruffles, tint other third of Clown Cream pale green with **green food color;** use in **decorating bag,** with **tube no. 112.**

7. Into peak of hat, push **2 large marshmallows.** With some pale-yellow frosting, fill in hat. Then use rest in **decorating bag,** with **tube no. 28,** to outline marshmallows and make hatband and pompons on shoes.

8. Cut 2 slices from **a small, round black gumdrop;** with scissors, snip 5 or 6 points in each. Use, cut side up as eyes. Split **1 oblong red gumdrop;** trim one half to 1½″ length, as mouth; use bit of other one for nose.

9. Center cake on **oblong plate** on party table. Circle with **glasses of pink lemonade.**

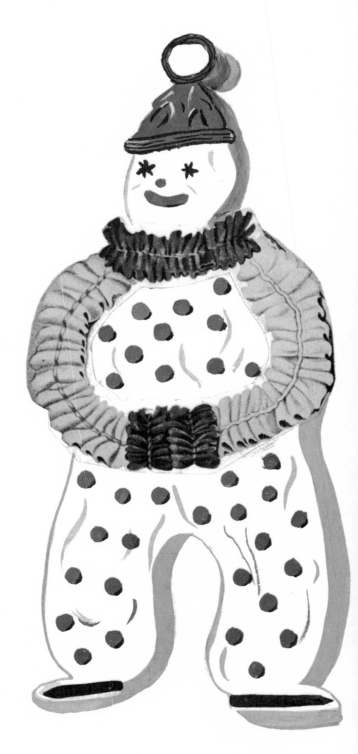

Anchors-Aweigh Cakes

Why not give today's bathtub sailors a party with a nautical air? Our fleet of cakes, afloat on sparkling "water," and with sails set to catch the breeze, is ideal for a child's outdoor party. Cut invitations in sailboat shapes, and word them in this fashion: "Commodore (name of honored sailor); Harbor (place where party is to be held); Number of Bells (time that party starts)."

Sailmaking:

This may be done days ahead. On **heavy white paper**, draw six large triangular sails, each with a 3½" base and 5¾" sides, and six small triangular sails, each with a 2½" base and one perpendicular 5" side; connect the two lines on each small sail with a curved line. Cut out sails.

On **sea-green paper**, draw six pennants, each 1½" by ½"; notch one end. On each, write name of invited young sailor; cut out.

With **cellophane tape**, fasten pennants to ends of **six colored 8½" drinking straws**; directly below each, attach large sail, then small one. Have sails all turned in same direction.

Boatbuilding:

Make up **1 large pkg. cake mix**; pour into two 8" layer-cake pans, or one 13" x 9" x 2" pan; bake as directed; cool.

On **cardboard**, draw 5" vertical line; in middle of it, center a 2¼" horizontal line. Connect four points with curved lines; cut out. With this pattern as base, make **five more cardboard bases**; wrap in foil.

Leaving ¼" between bases, arrange cardboard bases on cakes or cake. With sharp knife, cut around each base, down through cake. Carefully remove boat-shaped cakes; place each on cardboard base.

Getting Shipshape:

Make up **1 pkg. fluffy-white-frosting mix** as directed. Mix ¾ cup frosting with **1 tablesp. sifted cocoa;** use to frost cake tops (decks). Frost sides of boats with white frosting; decorate each with **round lime or colored candies** (we used 36).

Launching:

On **sea-green paper** in center of party table, line up boats. With **chalk**, draw waves. Set sails in place. At desserttime, each sailor selects boat with his name to eat.

Sassy Snowman

Day before:

Bake a **10″ tube angel food** from mix; cool. Make up **1 large pkg. yellow cake mix;** use to half fill a greased, floured, 3-cup oven-glass mixing bowl; into greased, floured, 6-cup oven-glass bowl, pour rest of batter. Bake cakes together at 350° F. 1 hr., or till done. In bowls on rack, cool cakes 15 min.; then remove; cool; wrap in foil.

On the day:

1. Make **Ornamental Frosting,** p. 177.

2. For body: Cover **11″ cardboard circle** with **foil.** With frosting, "glue" 6-cup bowl cake, inverted, to center. Then "glue" 3-cup bowl cake, inverted, on top. Trim to shape of snowman if necessary.

3. From angel food, cut wedge of cake 5″ across back; mold into 4″ ball; "glue" to body, as head. Lightly frost snowman.

4. Cut **5¼″ by 1¾″ pkg. of licorice twist** in half, for hat brim. For crown, bend **another pkg. of licorice** until ends meet; fasten with short picks. Stand crown on brim; secure with picks inserted from inside. Refrigerate.

5. Frost snowman again. Insert **round black gumdrop** eyes, **red oblong gumdrop** nose, a pipe of **licorice.** Sprinkle head with **coarsely crushed lump sugar.** Adjust hat at angle.

6. With **blue food color,** tint ½ cup frosting light blue. Use in **decorating bag,** with **tube no. 6,** to make waistcoat, buttons.

4. **For snowflakes on body:** In **decorating bag,** with **tube no. 30** and white frosting, make flakes, placing so they touch. Insert **4″ pieces from 2 candy canes** as arms; for scarf, use **red ribbon.**

8. Cut rest of angel food into 10 equal wedges. Remove top crust, then gently mold each into snowball; frost. Group around snowman; identify each with name of one of guests, using **decorating bag with tube no. 4,** and blue frosting.

9. Set on table; tuck **greens** here and there. At ice cream time, each guest enjoys his snowball, while Sassy Snowman looks on.

Peter Rabbit and Sons

You'll Need: Two 8″ or 9″ layers of Deep-Dark Chocolate Cake, p. 171, or Budget Gold Cake, p. 170, or your favorite cake mix or bakers' cake; Snow Peak, p. 178, or Yummy Chocolate Frosting, p. 179; large marshmallows; new paintbrush; food colors; birthday candles; cake plate.

Frosting and Decorating: Fill cake layers with some Snow Peak, tinted if you wish, or with Yummy Chocolate Frosting. Set layers on cake plate. Frost top and sides.

For each bunny, on side of cake, press 2 marshmallows, one above other, into frosting. For ears, split a marshmallow crosswise into two thinner circles; cut one of these circles in half; then pull each half a little to give ear effect; press into place on frosting so that ears just show above top of cake. For arms and legs, snip other marshmallow circle into little snippets; press into place where each should go.

Now dip paintbrush into bottle of red or green food color; paint eyes, mouth, nose, line on ears, and clothes, on each rabbit if you wish, as shown. Set two birthday candles in middle of cake, with third tall one to grow on.

Five-O'Clock Cake

You'll Need: Two 8″ or 9″ cake layers, made from favorite cake mix, bakers', or Heavenly Orange, Deep-Dark Chocolate, or Harlequin Cake, p. 171 and 172; No-Cook Marshmallow Frosting, p. 177, or Dreamy Frosting, p. 176; coarsely chopped walnuts; 13 black gumdrops; 2 long black gumdrop sticks; tiny candles; cake plate.

Frosting and Decorating: Put cake layers together with some of frosting; place on cake plate. Completely frost sides and top of cake. Into sides press chopped walnuts or pecans.

Place 1 black gumdrop on very center of cake; then, around top edge of cake, place 12 gumdrops as candleholders, with candle first stuck in each (see opposite). Place 2 long gumdrops in position to form hour and minute hands of clock, letting them point to the age of the birthday child.

Or use same number of candles as birthday child's age, placing them on appropriate gumdrop hours.

Candleholders: With point of sharp knife, cut crisscross gash in top of each gumdrop. Press candle into opening until it stands steady.

Coconut Characters

SNOW MAN

You'll Need: Four 8″ cake layers made from favorite cake mix, or Budget Gold Cake, p. 170, or from bakers'; Snow Peak, p. 178; flaked coconut; semisweet-chocolate pieces; red candy ball; gumdrops; chocolate cupcake; foil; chocolate peppermint candies; big candle, in birthday child's favorite color; cardboard circle or cake plate.

Foundation: Place first cake layer on cardboard circle, cut to fit. Cut second layer smaller than first layer, third layer smaller than second, fourth layer smaller than third.

Now "glue" layers together with Snow Peak. Then, with hands, form 2 cups cake crumbs (made from cake cuttings) mixed with a tablespoon or so of Snow Peak into cake-crumb ball; set in place on center of top cake layer as snow man's head.

Frosting and Decorating: Frost snow man with Snow Peak, then sprinkle him all over with flaked coconut. Use semisweet-chocolate pieces for his eyes, candy ball for his mouth, gumdrops for both nose and buttons. Arrange chocolate-cupcake hat at jaunty angle. Tie on scarf of foil, looping it once. Add chocolate-peppermint ear muffs, then big candle.

BUNNY

You'll Need: Four cake layers cut as for Snow Man, above; cake-crumb ball for tail and head; Snow Peak, p. 178; flaked coconut; long oval foil strips; pink straws; gumdrops; semisweet-chocolate pieces.

Frosting and Decorating: Completely frost bunny with Snow Peak; then sprinkle it all over with flaked coconut. Insert long foil ears, straw whiskers, gumdrop eyes and nose. Add semisweet-chocolate pieces for buttons.

Ice-Cream Log

You'll Need: Two ice-cream jelly rolls (kind you buy); Chocolate Chip Whipped Cream, p. 176; red candles; candied cherries; few small green leaves; long, narrow wooden board.

Frosting and Decorating: Place ice-cream jelly rolls, end to end, on the wooden board. Frost them all over with Chocolate Chip Whipped Cream. Then, run the flat side of a knife along frosted roll in parallel lines to simulate the bark on a log. Push each red candle into a candied cherry. Set securely, in a row, on the log. Tuck in some leaves.

Horseshoe Cake

Party Dress

Shaping boot: Make, bake, cool cake as in Window Garden, p. 118. Cut off 9″ length; stand up on crust end; shape back, front, and top as shown. From rest of cake, shape toe. On foil-covered cardboard, cut to fit, skewer pieces together.

Decorating it: Make 1½ batches Butter Cream, p. 175. Now tint ½ cup green; to 1 cup, add 2 tablesp. cocoa; with rest, frost cake. With cocoa frosting in decorating bag and tube no. 47, make sole and heel; then decorate both sides of boot with walnut halves, tiny red candies, silver dragées. With green frosting and tube no. 3, outline decorations. For spur, glue 2 foil stars together with end of toothpick between; insert in heel. Then add pebble candy as shown.

Buckaroo Boot

Prince Charming's Castle

Three how-to's for Prince Charming's Castle

1. Using heavy paper and Scotch tape, make 6 cylinders — 1 2¾″ high x 1½″ diameter, 1 3½″ x 1½″, 1 5″ x 1½″, 1 2¼″ x 2½″, 2 1¾″ x 1″. Make 6 cones — 3 3″ high x 2″ base, 2 2″ x 1½″, 1 3½″ x 3¼″. Notch base of widest cone at 3 points as seen center, below. For turrets, tape each cone to its match-ing cylinder, Frost all with Butter Cream (page 175); sprinkle tops with red and yellow sugar as pictured.

2. From colored paper, cut 3 pennants; tape to toothpicks; insert in 3 turrets. Center notched turret on frosted cake; fit 3 tallest turrets into notches. Place re-maining 2 turrets, sugar-tablet battle-ments, as shown.

3. For portcullis, press 5 cinnamon sticks against cake as pictured. To 2 tablesp. re-served Butter Cream, add 2 teasp. cocoa; use with no. 4 tube in paper cone to out-line door, battlements. Complete as on page 51.

60

Fairy Godmother   *Pumpkin Coach*   *Cinderella*

Three how-to's for Pumpkin Coach

1. To shape Pumpkin Coach: With sharp knife, make slanting cut in edge of unfrosted cake about ½" deep. Then round off edge by cutting away cake, all around rim, as shown below. Next turn cake upside down; repeat cutting at bottom edge to complete pumpkin shape.

2. To make ridges in coach: Lightly draw spatula (1½" wide) upward, in parallel strokes, from bottom to top of freshly frosted cake as shown below. Into hole at top of cake, insert cardboard circle to fit; spread with frosting. Complete decorating as in steps 2 and 3 of Pumpkin Coach (page 51).

3. To make wheels: From cardboard, cut 2 4¼" and 2 3½" circles; "paint" with chocolate Butter Cream (leftover from castle) or brown crayon. With white Butter Cream (leftover from castle) in no. 4 tube in paper cone, outline wheels and spokes. Add green-frosting decoration.

61

Birthday Limited

4 bakers' poundcakes,
  4" by 3"
1 bakers' jelly roll,
  5" by 4"
Large marshmallows
Chocolate Snow Peak,
  p. 178
Snow Peak, p. 178
1 set of food colors
Posie Cream, p. 177
Star tube, no. 28
Decorating bags

Plain tube for writing,
  no. 4
Large gumdrops
Semisweet chocolate
  pieces
Licorice sticks
Hard peppermint candy
Chocolate kiss
  (foil-wrapped)
Animal candleholders
  and candles

Coal Car and Engine:

For Coal Car, stand a poundcake with long side facing you. From left end, cut out rectangle 2½" by 1½", not quite to bottom. Set rectangle on top of back end of jelly-roll En-gine, as shown; secure with picks. Add marshmallow smokestack. Place Engine in front of Coal Car. Set on cardboard to fit.

Caboose:

Stand second poundcake with long side facing you. From either end, 1" up from bottom, cut out a rectangle 3" x 1" x 1". Split one rectangle lengthwise into 2 triangular blocks, as shown. Place one of triangular blocks on top. Set on cardboard to fit.

Animal Cars:

Slice each of remaining poundcakes into 3 flat crosswise slices. Place each, flat side down, on cardboard to fit.

62

Frosting and Decorating:

Make up a batch of Chocolate Snow Peak, as directed. Use it to frost Engine and Coal Car; then use any leftover frosting on one or more of the Animal Cars. Make up a batch of Snow Peak, as directed; then frost the Caboose with one third of it, tinted pink with food color. Use rest of Snow Peak, tinted if desired, to frost rest of cars. Now, make up a batch of white or tinted Posie Cream; use with star tube in decorating bag to trim train. Then switch to plain tube to write name of each child guest on side of each car.

Press on split marshmallows and gumdrops for wheels. With Posie Cream, "glue" on a semisweet-chocolate piece for the center of each wheel. "Glue" on licorice for the cow-catcher, wheel rods, caboose railing. Press on a peppermint candy for the headlight, a chocolate kiss on a toothpick for the Engine bell. Use semisweet-chocolate pieces for coal.

Chug Along:

Place train, in winding line, along table. Set animal candleholders and candles atop each car. Sprinkle multicolored candy or colored sugar for road-bed. The clown is climbing up a tall candle set in the center of the table.

63

SWANEE

At a birthday party it's pure delight
To bring out this cake . . . cut-up right.
Swanee's beak is gumdrop yellow
Wouldn't it please a little fellow?

SPOT, the Fox Terrier

This Fox Terrier's name is Spot,
He's the friskiest in the lot.
Whip him up with your favorite mix,
Add coconut spots and teach him tricks!

SAILIN' DOWN THE BAY

SWANEE

1. Measure down 4 inches at corners, 1½ inches at middle of cool 13 x 9 x 2 inch cake. Cut on a curve at points of long side. Cut off corners for tail and head.

2. From a corner on remaining piece, measure 3½ inches along short side, 5½ inches across long side. Cut through points on curve to form swan's wing.

3. Place pieces as shown. Spread fluffy white frosting over cake. Shake on lots of snowy white flaked coconut for Swanee's feathers. Swanee's eye is a gumdrop, the beak, gumdrop strips.

SPOT, the Fox Terrier

1. Bake a 13 x 9 x 2-inch cake. Cool. Cut out a 10 x 3-inch rectangle. Then cut off a 4-inch piece and divide remaining piece in half. Cut a narrow strip from L-shaped piece for tail.

2. Assemble pieces on tray as shown. Spread a fluffy seven minute frosting generously over cake. Pat toasted flaked coconut on part of head and back of dog for brown spots.

3. Now sprinkle on snowy white flaked coconut for Spot's coat. His eyes and nose are gumdrops, licorice makes his mouth and a sculptured cookie his ear. His collar is made from Licorice, silver dragées and cut green gumdrops.

SAILIN' DOWN THE BAY

1. For this sailboat bake a 9-inch square cake from any cake mix. When cool, cut cake diagonally in half to make two triangles. One is the large sail. From the other, cut off a strip 2¼ inches wide to use for the hull.

2. Arrange cake pieces on tray, as shown, using small triangle as the second sail. Spread white butter cream frosting on sails and cover hull with chocolate frosting.

3. Make your sailboat look truly nautical! Put a line of chocolate frosting between the sails for the mast. Then sprinkle flaked coconut generously over the sails. White candies make neat portholes . . . and gumdrops are easily cut into an anchor and a crescent for the sail.

Four Shining Angels

(pictured on p. 73)

PARASOL SHOWER CAKE

Tint **Snow Peak, p. 178,** pink. Use to frost **10″ angel cake.** Anchor **15″ candle** on **flower-holder;** to bottom, press **½″ putty ball;** press in place in center of cake. Stick **7 opened, variegated, tiny paper parasols** into cake. To candle top, tie **twelve 27″ lengths of variegated ribbons;** wrap three around candle. To candle top and also under its ribbon, attach an **opened parasol.**

CANDLEWICK BIRTHDAY CAKE

1. Snip edges of **minature marshmallows** equidistantly 5 times. **Tint Snow Peak, p. 178, pale yellow.** Reserve ¼ cup; use rest to frost **10″ angel cake.**

2. Break **8 tongue blades (from druggist)** in half; equidistantly around cake, 1″ below top edge, insert 8 pieces horizontally, with ½″ sticking out; between every two blades, 1½″ below top edge, insert another. To flat end of each blade, "glue" **candle** with **melted wax.** Set marshmallows on cake; with frosting, glue

3 to each candle.

DAD'S BIRTHDAY GINGERBREAD CAKE

1. Roll **ginger-cookie dough** ⅛″ **thick.** With **cardboard pattern,** cut out **7 gingerbread men, 3″ high,** and **a 7 point star** with 1½″ circle cut from center. On men arrange **currants.** Bake, cool. With **Snow Peak, p. 178,** frost a **10″ angel cake** made from mix.

2. Mix ⅔ **cup sifted confectioners' sugar** with **2 teasp. water;** use with **plain tube no. 5** to decorate star and men. Set star on cake, men around sides.

FASHIONABLE FEATHER PARTY CAKE

1. With **food color,** tint ½ **cup Snow Peak p. 178,** pink; ½ **cup, light green;** ½ **cup, light blue.** Use rest to frost **10″ angel cake.**

2. Use **pink frosting** in **decorating bag,** with **plain tube no. 7.** Starting 1½″ below cake center, press out V shape in 2 strokes. Repeat Vs, one under the other, each slightly more to left, to complete feather. Make next feather green, next blue; repeat around cake.

And One to Grow On

(pictured on p. 74)

One 10″ angel food or chiffon cake
Snow Peak, p. 178
Set of food colors

3 ½ cups flaked coconut
Tiny pink, yellow, green candles
Cakeplate

Day before, if desired:

Make cake from mix or favorite recipe. Cool, remove from pan, wrap in foil, store.

On the day:

1. Set unwrapped cake on cake plate. Frost top and sides with Snow Peak.

2. Tint 1½ cups flaked coconut green, 1 cup pink, 1 cup yellow, as on p. 10. Sprinkle on cake in panels, alternating colors.

3. Then group candles on matching panels.

66

Pink Petal Cake

(pictured on p. 75)

2 8″ or 9″ cake layers
from cake mix, or
Budget Gold,
Heavenly Orange,
Deep Dark Chocolate,
or Harlequin Cake,
p. 170, 171, or 172
One batch Snow Peak,
p. 178, tinted pale
yellow

One batch Snow Peak,
p. 178, part tinted
pale green, rest
delicate pink
Food colors
Silver dragées, (tiny
silver coated candy
balls)
Candleholders
Candles
Cake plate

Day before, if desired:

Make and bake cake layers, cool, remove from pans, wrap, then store.

On party day:

1. Make 2 batches Snow Peak; tint one batch pale yellow; tint part of other batch pale green, and rest very delicate pink.

2. On **cake plate**, use yellow Snow Peak to fill and frost top and sides of layers. Then, with **teaspoon**, drop about 9 mounds of green Snow Peak, spoke-fashion, around outer top edge of cake to resemble leaves. (In doing this, gently shake frosting off side of spoon, making oval leaf shape; let leaves go right to edge of cake.)

3. Now, with **another spoon,** drop big fat mounds of pink frosting between and on top of green leaves, about 1″ in from edge of cake. Top these with a few more pink petals.

4. Tint rest of pink frosting a shade or so deeper. Place spoonful in center of flower; with back of spoon, spread to form open center petals, pulling up little points here and there. Sprinkle with silver dragées.

5. Lastly, bend the wire of each candleholder so it is at right angles to candle. Insert around sides of cake, near top.

6. Light and take to the birthday child, to be served with tea, coffee, or milk.

Family Portrait for Dad

(pictured on p. 76)

2 Chocolate Sheet
Cakes, p. 171; or
two 13″ x 9″ x 2″
sheet cakes made
from cake mix
Two batches Yummy
Chocolate Frosting,
p. 179
Apricot jam

Artist's palette
Confectioners' sugar
Instant coffee
Plain tube for writing,
no. 4
Decorating bag
Food colors
Taper candles

Day before, if desired:

Make chocolate sheet cakes; cool, remove from pans, wrap, then store until needed next day.

On the day:

1. Make the two batches of Yummy Chocolate Frosting.

2. Put two cakes together, using apricot jam as filling. Set cake on new artist's palette (cake server becomes artist's brush); or use a rectangular board, or glass cake plate, if you have no palette. Frost top and sides of filled cake with Yummy Chocolate Frosting.

3. To about 1 cup sifted confectioners' sugar, add small amount of water, mixing it in, a few drops at a time, until of spreading consistency. To half of this, add small amount of instant coffee; use, in **decorating bag,** with **plain tube for writing, no. 4,** to draw the family of stick figures, and write "Happy Birthday Dad," as our picture shows.

4. Divide other half of white frosting into thirds; tint some pink, some yellow, some green. Using **tube for writing, no. 4,** and **decorating bag** of frosting, fill in Mom's pink apron, big brother's green pants, Helen's yellow skirt and hair ribbon.

5. Give each figure a taper candle, cut to make steplike row, as pictured. Fido, as you will note, balances a small candle on his nose.

Note: If you aren't having a big party, you may find that just one chocolate cake is enough to decorate.

Corsage Cake

You'll Need: A 9″ or 10″ tube angel, chiffon or sponge cake, made from mix or your own recipe, or from the bakers'; food colors; Snow Peak, p. 178, tinted pale pink or green; silver dragées; tiny pink or green candles; old-fashioned nosegay of fresh flowers; cake plate.

Frosting, Decorating: Frost cake with pale-pink or green Snow Peak; sprinkle on silver dragées. Ring top edge with candles. Set nosegay (birthday child may wear it) in center.

Lollipop Cake

You'll Need: A 9″ or 10″ tube angel, sponge or chiffon cake; Snow Peak, p. 178; large gumdrops; wooden skewers; lace-paper doily; yellow candles; cake plate.

Frosting, Decorating: Frost cake with Snow Peak. Make lollipops by inserting wooden skewer in each of 9 gumdrops. Remove center from paper doily; insert lollipops; tie with ribbon. Set in cake center. Ring with candles.

Conversation Piece

You'll Need: Four 6″ or 8″ layer cakes, from cake mix or bakers', or Heavenly Orange Cake, p. 172; Snow Peak, p. 178; food colors; plain tube for writing, no. 4; decorating bag; ribbon or string for hatbox; tiny birthday candles; medium corks; assorted tiny artificial blossoms with leaves; straight pins; round cake plate, wooden board or mirror.

Frosting and Decorating: "Glue" 4 cake layers together with some of Snow Peak; set them on cake plate. Frost smoothly three fourths the way up side with half of remaining Snow Peak.

Then tint rest of Snow Peak deep pink; use with **plain tube for writing** and **decorating bag** to make up-and-down stripes, about 1″ apart, around side of cake. Frost top of cake, then one fourth way down side, with more pink Snow Peak, spreading it smooth to resemble hatbox cover.

Tint rest of frosting deeper pink; use, with **plain tube for writing** and **decorating bag,** to write fashionable lady's name on top. Across top, place hatbox ribbon or string; tie in bow; tuck ends of ribbon into side of frosted cake.

Candleholders: Slightly melt ends of tiny candles; set one in place on top of each cork. Cut stems off tiny blossoms; insert pin through center of each; insert into top and sides of corks to form clusters. Tuck leaves (on pins) here and there. Set candles, one for each guest, around hatbox cake.

Butterfly Cake

You'll Need: Two 8″ or 9″ white cake layers; jam; rectangular board or cake plate; Butter Cream, p. 175; 8″ or 9″ paper doily with plain center; cocoa; decorating bag; plain tube for writing, no. 4; colored pipe cleaners.

Frosting and Decorating: Fill cake layers with jam, then cut in halves. Set, with rounded sides touching, and slightly at an angle, on board. Reserve ⅓ cup Butter Cream; use rest to frost top and sides of cake halves. Then lay half a paper doily on top of each, and sift cocoa over entire top. Now lift off doily, leaving its pattern, in cocoa, on top.

Add **a little melted, unsweetened chocolate** to reserved frosting; use, with **decorating bag,** and **tube no. 4,** to add name of birthday child. Affix pipe cleaners as antennae.

A Tie for His Birthday

You'll Need: Chocolate Sheet Cake, p. 171, or 13″ x 9″ x 2″ cake made from favorite cake mix or recipe; Snow Peak, p. 178; food colors; plain tube for writing, no. 4; decorating bags, p. 11; oval cake plate or wooden board.

Making Tie: From **paper or lightweight cardboard,** cut out a bow-tie pattern, making the tie large enough to cover entire surface of a 13″ x 9″ x 2″ cake. Set cake on cake plate.

Now lay the pattern on top of cake; with sharp knife, trace around it, cutting through to bottom of cake; trim where needed. From cut pieces, make 2 loose ends of bow tie; set in place. (Or, before cutting, place cake in flat, waxed-paper-lined box that resembles tie box in shape and size.)

Frosting and Decorating: Completely frost bow tie with Snow Peak. Tint rest of frosting pink; use, with **tube no. 4, in decorating bag,** to make pink stripes and outline tie.

If He Prefers a Four-in-Hand:

You'll Need: One 10″ x 5″ x 3″ loaf cake made from your favorite cake mix, or a Harlequin Loaf, p. 172; Orange Dreamy Frosting, p. 176; food colors; plain tube for writing, no. 4; decorating bag.

Frosting and Decorating: Frost cake, reserving a little for tie stripes; tint this green. With **wooden pick,** outline on frosting a full length, four-in-hand necktie of same length as cake. Using **tube no. 4,** in **decorating bag** and green frosting, outline tie; then make stripes, placing those on knot in one direction, rest in other direction.

Club-Party Cake

You'll Need:	7" and 10" Pans	13" Pan
Sifted cake flour	3½ cups	4¼ cups plus 2 tablesp.
Double-acting baking powder	4 teasp.	5 teasp.
Salt	1 teasp.	1¼ teasp.
Soft shortening*	1 cup	1¼ cups
Granulated sugar	2 cups	2½ cups
Eggs	4	5
Milk	1 cup	1¼ cups
Vanilla extract	1 teasp.	1¼ teasp.

Also 2 batches Maple Snow Peak, p. 178; 5" candle; daisies.

On day before: Grease, line with waxed paper, bottoms of 3 pans of tier cake set above. Start heating oven to 350° F.

Make batter for 7" and 10" pans this way: Sift flour with baking powder, salt. In large bowl, with mixer at medium speed, mix shortening with sugar, then with eggs, one at a time, until very light, fluffy—about 4 min. At low speed, beat in flour mixture alternately with milk and extract, beating just until smooth. Turn batter into 7" and 10" pans, filling not quite half-full. Bake 7" pan 45 min., 10" pan 55 min., or until cake tester comes out clean. Cool in pans on wire racks 5 min. Remove from pans; peel off papers; cool. Store in waxed paper.

For 13" pan, use ingredients listed in last column; bake 70 min., or until done; cool; wrap; store.

On the day: Set 13" layer on large round tray; frost top and side. Top with 10" layer; frost top and side. Set 7" layer on top; frost top and side, mounding frosting a bit on top. Set candle in center of top; arrange daisies as shown.

---

* Any brand that comes in 1- or 3-lb. can.

Dad's Birthday Pie

You'll Need: Favorite apple pie; process cheese, soft enough to mold; paprika; candles; huckleberry leaves; tray.

Decorating: Just before baking pie, with sharp knife, cut words "Happy Birthday" in top crust. After baking, set warm pie on a large round tray—a wooden one, perhaps.

For Candle Apples: Mold each 1" cube of process cheese into crab-apple shape; add blush by dipping one side of each "apple" in paprika; insert candle in each; tuck in small green leaf. Arrange 8 "apples" around pie.

Toothsome Telegram

You'll Need: Applesauce Cake, p. 170, or Chocolate Sheet Cake, p. 171, or 13″ x 9″ x 2″ cake made from favorite recipe or cake mix; Dreamy Frosting, p. 176; instant coffee; plain tube for writing, no. 4; decorating bag; candles; narrow ribbon; an oblong cake plate or wooden board.

On day before: Make and bake cake, as recipe directs. Cool it, remove from pan, then wrap and store it until needed the next day.

On the day: Set cake on cake plate or wooden board. Make Dreamy Frosting, then frost top and sides of cake with some of it. To remaining frosting, add a little instant coffee, and stir until well blended.

Use this frosting, with plain tube for writing no. 4, in decorating bag, to duplicate the heading on a telegram blank on the cake, and then to write the birthday telegram message, as shown. Add two candles and ribbon frills as finishing touches.

For a Special Year

You'll Need: Chocolate Sheet Cake, p. 171; 2 Gold Square Cakes, p. 171; or favorite cake mix baked in two 9″ x 9″ x 2″ pans or a 13″ x 9″ x 2″ pan; food colors; Snow Peak, p. 178, tinted favorite color of birthday child; Posie Cream, p. 177; rose-petal tube no. 127; leaf tube no. 68; decorating bags; rectangular cake plate or mirror.

For Numbers: Draw **large paper or cardboard pattern** for each numeral of special year, making them as large as the sheet cake or two 9″ x 9″ x 2″ cakes permit. Place first pattern on top of cake; with sharp knife, carefully trace around it, cutting through to bottom of cake; remove excess cake. Then cut out second cake numeral, in same way, using other part of sheet cake or second square cake.

Frosting and Decorating: Place cake numerals side by side on mirror or cake plate. Frost with Snow Peak; then, on each numeral, spoon mound of frosting just where you plan to place the roses. Remove small amount of Posie Cream to small bowl; tint green; set aside for leaves.

Then, use rest of white Posie Cream, tinted pink perhaps, to make a few roses and rosebuds, as in **Susan's Posies, p. 28.** Arrange on each cake number, as shown. Then, with leaf tube no. 68 in decorating bag, and green Posie Cream, tuck green leaves here and there.

71

Take a Cake

TICKTACKTOE

Frost your favorite **9″ x 9″ x 2″ cake** with **Snow Peak, p. 178.** Then, outline 2″ squares over frosted surface by drizzling on **melted unsweetened chocolate** thinned with **a little corn syrup.** Now set **tiny yellow candles** diagonally across top of cake; then place **gumdrop rings,** cut side up, and **tiny candy balls** or **gumdrops** as shown.

ROLY POLY

Make favorite **jelly roll;** or buy two from baker and set end to end. Make **Snow Peak, p. 178;** reserve ⅓ cup; tint rest pale green. Use green frosting to frost jelly roll. Then add a **little melted chocolate** to reserved frosting and use in **decorating bag,** with **plain tube for writing no. 4** to write each guest's first name across top of roll.

STENCIL CAKE

For stencil, cut **circle of paper to fit top of cake;** cut out **initials** of **birthday child.** Frost cake with **dark butter frosting.** Then gently place stencil on top; sift **confectioners' sugar** over cut out portion; then lift off stencil. Or try sifting **instant cocoa mix, instant coffee,** or **cinnamon-sugar mixture** onto light frosting. Or instead of initials make stencil of birthday age.

Four

Shining

Angels

And One To Grow On

Pink Petal Cake

Family Portrait for Dad

Coconut Kitten

3 large pkg. yellow cake mix
Foil
Cardboard oblong, 15″ by 10″
Wooden skewers
1½ batches Snow Peak, p. 178
Food colors
Flaked coconut

1 batch Snow Cream, p. 178
Decorating bags
Decorating tubes, no. 27, 3
Ball, 1″ in diameter
4 pointed paper cups
Toothpicks
Semisweet chocolate pieces

On day before, if desired:

1. Make, bake, cool 1 pkg. cake mix in two 8″ layer pans.

2. Then grease and line with waxed paper a 15½″ x 10½″ x 2½″ roasting pan. Prepare 2 pkg. cake mix, one after the other, as label directs, pouring into pan. Bake at 350° F. 55 min., or until cake tester inserted in center comes out clean.

3. Cool cake in pan on rack; invert on foil-covered cardboard oblong (it's to be kitten's pillow); remove waxed paper.

Early on party day:

1. Halve one 8″ cake layer crosswise; stand on cut ends, side by side and in a diagonal position, on the pillow.

2. For tail, from around outer edge of other layer, cut 1″-wide strip, 7″ long; with skewers, fasten it at back.

3. For paws, from same layer, cut 2 pieces, each 4″ long, 1½″ wide at one end, and tapering to nothing at other end; place at front, tapered ends out, and slightly apart, as shown.

4. For head, cut 3″ circle from cake; stand it up on paws, turned slightly to kitten's left; fasten in place with skewer.

5. Frost kitten with about half of Snow Peak. With spatula, at sides of head, pull up frosting to make ears. With food color, tint a little frosting pale pink, then use for inside of ears; tint a little blue, and use to make slanted eyes.

6. With coconut, generously sprinkle kitten, except for inside of ears and eyes; brush off any that falls on pillow.

7. Tint rest of Snow Peak pink; carefully frost pillow on sides and over top around kitten, making ridges with spatula for plumped effect. Set in place, on oblong board if desired, on table.

8. Tint Snow Cream deep pink; use **in decorating bag, with tube no. 27,** to make cording all around top edges of pillow.

9. On pillow, place ball as shown; on ball, with pink Snow Cream and tube no. 3, press out rows of frosting in yarn effect. Now for tassel, cut 1½″-deep tip from each of 4 paper cups; press pointed end of each tip up into a corner of pillow. On each, with same tube, make vertical rows of frosting; **with tube no. 27,** add a rosette at top.

10. Give kitten toothpick whiskers (3 on each side); a mouth of halved semisweet pieces; eyes of a bit of semisweet.

Bûche de Noël
(pictured on p. 85)

Bûche de Noël Roll,
  p. 170
Chocolate Butter
  Cream, p. 175

Cake plate
Glacéed fruit, p. 00
Fresh green leaves

Early on the day:

1. Make Bûche de Noël Roll; cool.

2. Make Chocolate Butter Cream; cover until ready to use.

3. Unroll cooled chocolate roll; spread surface with 1 cup Chocolate Butter Cream. Carefully reroll, lifting towel higher and higher with one hand as you guide with other.

4. Place, seam side down, on serving plate. Under each of log's long sides tuck strip of waxed paper so it extends about 2″.

5. On top of log, about 2″ from one end and off center, lay two 1½″ strips of reserved cake, end to end, in oval knot. Secure with toothpicks. Thinly frost entire surface of log with Chocolate Butter Cream.

6. Next, with a little frosting, and **tube no. 47 in decorating bag,** make "bark" effect on log in this way: Hold tube at about 45° angle to surface of log; then start a light pressure, moving the tube forward and slightly upward. As tube is brought to end of each ¾″-long piece of "bark," decrease pressure and quickly raise tube straight up, breaking off flow of frosting. Repeat, covering entire surface of log, while conforming to contour of log, as pictured. Also fill in the knot.

7. Remove waxed-paper strips. Refrigerate cake. To serve, garnish with glacéed fruit and leaves. Slice, removing picks.

New Year's Marshmallow Chocolate Cake
(pictured on p. 86)

Marshmallow Chocolate
  Cake, p. 172
6 tablesp. butter
1 cup brown sugar,
  packed
¼ cup light cream

1 cup chopped walnuts
2 6¼-oz. pkg. miniature
  marshmallows
Chocolate Butter
  Frosting, p. 176
Cake stand

Early on the day:

1. Make, bake, cool 3 cake layers.

2. In small bowl, with mixer at medium speed, thoroughly blend butter, sugar, cream; mix in nuts. Spread top of each of three layers with one-third of this topping. Then, on top of each, arrange marshmallows side by side, close together.

3. Broil, about 6″ from heat, just until lightly browned. Cool thoroughly.

4. Now, on pretty cake stand, lay four 2″-wide waxed-paper strips in square. Stack marshmallow-topped layers, one on other.

6. Frost sides with Chocolate Butter Frosting, making pretty diagonal swirls with spatula, as pictured. Remove waxed-paper. Serve in wedges.

Ring in the New

Grease, then flour, two 9″ by 8″ bell-shaped layer-cake pans. In them, bake and cool **1 large pkg. white-cake mix** as label directs. Repeat with **second pkg. white-cake mix.**

Meanwhile, trace outline of two 9″ by 8″, bell-shaped layer-cake pans on **cardboard.** Cut out shapes; cover with **foil;** fit one cake layer on each. Make up **1 large pkg. fluffy-white frosting mix,** adding 1 **teasp. almond extract.** Use to spread over layers on cardboard; top with second layers; lightly frost all over.

Make up **second pkg. fluffy-white-frosting mix,** use to refrost cakes, following contours of bells. Sprinkle tops with **silver dragées** as shown. Then cover sides of cakes with **flaked coconut** in snowy effect.

Arrange bells as party table centerpiece, with inner top sides just touching, and at an angle so they appear to be swinging away from each other. From **3 yd. of 2″ silver ribbon,** cut one 1 yd. streamer, another ½ yd. long. With rest of ribbon, make large bow.

Arrange streamers on outsides of bells; center bow on top with **toothpick.** Scatter **star confetti,** cut from varicolored construction paper, on and around ribbon.

Note: Lacking bell-shape pans, bake four 9″ cake layers. Make bell pattern by folding 8″ paper circle in half and trimming to bell shape. Lay opened bell pattern on each cake layer; with sharp knife, trim layer to match. Proceed as directed above.

New Year's Eve Cakes

Happy New Year:

1. Make your **favorite white, yellow or gold cake** in a sheet pan. When done, and cooled, cut into 2″ squares.

2. Frost 12 squares, on all sides, with **Snow Peak, p. 178**. With **silver dragées** (edible candy-coated balls), or **red-tinted sugar**, or **green-tinted Ornamental Frosting, p. 177**, in a **decorating bag**, with **tube no. 4**, form one of the letters of HAPPY NEW YEAR on each square.

3. Then group the letters on a tray to spell out the greeting. Tuck **spray of pine, evergreen**, or **mistletoe**, tied with a **silver ribbon** on both sides as shown.

Ring In The New Year

1. Set your **favorite filled chocolate layer cake** on an attractive **cake plate**. Frost it with **whipped cream**.

2. With **toothpick** outline a bell on the center top of the cake. Then, with **canned crushed pineapple**, well drained on paper towels, fill in outline of bell.

3. Place **maraschino cherry** in appropriate spot for clapper. Also use **snipped cherries** to outline bow at top of bell.

4. Cut the year from red construction paper. Paste on cake plate in front of cake. Encircle rest of plate with **mistletoe**. (With **yellow ribbon** tie a **few bells** to knife you use to cut cake.)

Variation: Frost **filled cake** with **Snow Peak**. Use **cut up maraschinos** to outline bell clapper and bow. Scatter **silver dragées** in the outline of bell. Sprinkle **flaked coconut** around bell on top and sides of cake.

The Clock Strikes Twelve:

Place **filled cake layers** on tray. **Frost in white.** Cream ½ **tablesp. butter or margarine** with ½ **cup confectioners' sugar** and about **1 teasp. cream**; tint red with drop of **food color.** Use in **decorating bag** with **plain tube for writing no. 4** to outline hours and hands of clock striking 12. Buy tiny **1″ by 1″ calendar**. Paste 12 months of year on plate around cake. To use cake as centerpiece, surround it with **clocks—five** are nice—**with** alarms set to go off at 12 o'clock. Weave **serpentine** or **Christmas-tree tinsel rope** around clocks.

To My Valentine

2¼ cups sifted cake
    flour
1½ cups granulated
    sugar
3 teasp. double-acting
    baking powder
1 teasp salt
½ cup salad oil
6 egg yolks, unbeaten

1 teasp. grated lemon
    rind
2 teasp. lemon juice
¾ cup water
6 egg whites
½ teasp. cream of
    tartar
Dreamy Frosting,
    p. 176

Bake cakes day before:

Start heating oven to 350° F. Into large bowl, sift first 4 ingredients; mix well. Add oil, yolks, rind, juice, water; with egg beater, beat smooth. In large bowl, with mixer at high speed, beat whites with cream of tartar, **very stiff;** fold in yolk mixture till just blended. Turn into **2 ungreased heart-shaped layer pans.** Bake 35 min., or until done. Invert to cool, resting edges on two other pans. Loosen all around with spatula; remove; trim overhang with scissors. Repeat, making 2 more heart layers.

Early on the day:

Make Dreamy Frosting; tint all but ¾ cup deep pink. Stack 2 heart layers. At their right, hold third layer, above, and overlapping their top 3″ at widest part. With knife, cut around overlap, down through 2 layers; remove cut pieces. Fill cut layers, then whole heart layers with pink frosting.

On **39″-by-12″ cardboard,** fit whole heart layers (at right) into cut set of layers (at left); trace around hearts; cut out **double heart of cardboard** and cover with **foil.** Also cut out **3 cardboard whole hearts;** stack these; cover with foil; place to right on double heart cardboard. Set cut-heart cake at left on cardboard, fit whole heart cake into it at right. Frost cakes pink. With white frosting, in **decorating bag,** and **rosette tube no. 28,** decorate tops as shown. Insert **taper candle** through cakes as arrow; tape **red-paper heart** to tip; tie **bow** on other end; circle with **roses, greens.**

Cakes for the Sentimental Season

Make these sweetheart cakes for a shut-in on Valentine's Day. Or use them as the **pièce de résistance** at a buffet supper. If you have a freezer, you may make cakes several days or weeks ahead, freezer wrap, and freeze. On the day, allow 1 hour for thawing, then frost.

LOVE YOU CAKE

2¼ cups sifted cake flour	½ cup soft shortening*
1½ cups granulated sugar	1 teasp. grated orange rind
¼ teasp. baking soda	¼ cup orange juice
1 teasp. salt	¾ cup water
3 teasp. double-acting baking powder	2 medium eggs, unbeaten

1. Start heating oven to 350° F. Grease, then line with waxed paper bottoms of two heart-shaped layer pans (5-cups capacity).

2. Into large bowl, sift first 5 ingredients. Drop in shortening, rind; pour in all but ⅓ cup combined orange juice and water. With mixer at low to medium speed, beat 2 min., scraping bowl, beaters, as needed.

3. Add eggs and rest of orange-juice mixture; beat 2 min. Turn into pans. Bake 30 min., or until cake tester, inserted in center of each layer, comes out clean. Cool in pans, on wire racks, 10 min. Remove from pans; peel off waxed paper; finish cooling.

* Any brand of shortening in 1- or 3-lb. cans.

To Serve on Valentine's Day:

1. When cakes have cooled, or thawed, trace outline of the two heart-shaped layer-cake pans on **cardboard.** Cut out shapes; cover with **foil;** then place one cake layer on each.

2. Now make **Carnation-Pink Frosting,** p. 175, and use to frost each layer generously.

3. With **red decorating jelly** (comes in a tube), write **Love** on one layer, **You** on other.

4. On a pretty tray, if for a shut-in, or the buffet if for a buffet supper, arrange three overlapping **heart-shape paper doilies** to make one larger heart.

5. Place one cake on doily heart. Repeat with three more doilies and other layer.

6. Now arrange **1″ red ribbon** around cakes and doilies, then **carnations** and **greens.**

82

Special Cakes for February

VALENTINE-MAILBOX CAKE

1. Split a **5" x 3" x 3" bakers' pound cake** into 2 layers; set side by side on **cardboard 7" by 6".** From center of two 7" sides, remove rectangle of cake 3" by 1". From center of two 6" sides, remove rectangle of cake 2" by 1".

2. Now, on top of **each** original layer, set **three 5" x 3" x 3" pound cakes.** Secure cakes together with **4 wooden skewers;** trim sides straight. Round off sides at top, as shown.

3. From front top of mailbox, cut out wedge-shaped piece, as shown, to simulate mailbox chute. Make **Butter Cream, p. 175.** Set aside about ⅓ cup; with **food colors,** tint one third of rest **red,** two-thirds **deep blue.** From bottom up, frost two-thirds of cake blue; rest red.

4. Using **plain tube no. 5** in **decorating bag,** with reserved white frosting, print "U.S. Mail" across front; add handle.

5. Around mailbox, arrange **addressed Valentines;** tuck one, held by **cupid-cutout,** near chute.

CHERRY-TREE CAKE

1. Day before, or early on the day, make, bake **two 9" white cake layers;** cool; wrap; store.

2. On party day, fill layers with **1 cup mashed canned jellied cranberry sauce.** Make up **1 pkg. fluffy white frosting mix;** tint ½ cup **royal blue;** use rest to frost cake.

3. With **plain tube no. 5** and blue frosting in **decorating bag,** write "I cannot tell a lie" around cake.

4. Insert **3 twigs** and **a tree stump** in top of cake; across top, lay **chopped-down tree.** With **thin wire,** hang **candied cherries** on twigs. Add **blue ribbon bows** and **7" toy hatchet.**

ABE'S STOVEPIPE-HAT CAKE

1. On 10½" **cardboard circle,** stack **three 6" bakers' angel** cakes. Trim sides of cakes straight; insert **3 wooden skewers** to fasten together. On top, place **4" cardboard circle.** With **Snow Peak, p. 178,** tinted brown, frost cake and cardboards.

2. Around base of cake, arrange about **13 thin square peppermint patties** as hatband. Set cake on **box top, about 12" x 12" x 1";** drape **row of red, white, and blue crepe-paper streamers** around it, catching them up at intervals with bits of red crepe paper to form scallops.

Coconut-Drifted Valentine

(pictured on p. 87)

Having a dinner party for sweethearts on this special day? We think this luscious coconut-drifted cake is just the perfect ending for such a party.

Or serve it, as the **pièce de résistance,** with coffee, to all sweethearts gathered for St. Valentine's Day fun.

Act I—Early on Valentine's Day:

Make, bake, and cool **two batches of Valentine Layer Cake, p. 174.**

Act II—Later the Same Day:

1. On **9″ foil-covered cardboard circle,** arrange three of cake layers, one over the other; fill and frost with **Sweetheart Frosting, p. 178.** (Freeze fourth layer for a later family dessert.)

2. Make paper frills for nosegays which circle cake: With scissors, cut **seven 8″ white paper doilies** in half. Bring two outer edges of each half-doily to center, so they overlap **slightly;** staple in place.

3. On cake plate, arrange frills, side by side, so that their rounded edges are just even with edge of plate; then anchor each with a bit of **cellophane tape.**

Act III—The Finale:

1. Carefully lift cardboard-backed frosted cake to **cake plate,** and set it in center of paper frills.

2. Cut stems of about **2 doz. pink garnet roses** to 2″ length. Save **a few pretty leaves.**

3. Now tuck roses into each paper frill, making an old-fashioned nosegay, as pictured. If necessary, add a few leaves here and there for accent.

4. Then set the Coconut-Drifted Valentine on a **pastel-pink cloth,** with **cake server, forks,** and **plates nearby.**

5. To duplicate our picture, arrange a large **bouquet of pink garnet roses** and a **deep-red candy jar** in the background. You can cut and serve each wedge of cake proudly, secure in the knowledge that it is as good to eat as it is to look at.

Easter Song

(pictured on p. 88)

Confetti Easter-Egg
  Cake, p. 171
Food colors
1 can flaked coconut;
  or green-paper grass
Cardboard; foil
½ batch Posie Cream,
  p. 177

1 batch pink-tinted
  Snow Peak, p. 178
Decorating bags
Rosette tube no. 28,
  and leaf tube no. 68
Jordan almonds or
  jelly beans; spring
  flowers, and ribbons

On day before:

1. Make and bake cake in two 3-cup mixing bowls described in cake recipe; store, covered. With green food color, tint coconut green; or tint small amounts of coconut different colors, then toss together.

2. Cut off corners of 11″ by 8½″ oblong of cardboard to make oval; cover with foil. Cut 3″ foil circle to use as window of egg.

On day of party:

1. Slice just enough from top of cakes to make surfaces flat. With Posie Cream, "glue" tops of cakes together to make egg shape; then cut narrow slice from one side of egg so it will rest steady. Set egg; cut side down, on foil-covered cardboard.

2. Using pink Snow Peak, and making lengthwise strokes with spatula, generously frost cake, building up egglike shape. Place 3″ foil circle at one end to resemble window.

3. With food colors, tint small amounts of Posie Cream pink, blue, yellow, and green. With these, 4 decorating bags, tube no. 28, and leaf tube no. 68, decorate around window, being sure to cover edges of foil.

4. Now set egg in place on table. For "nest," sprinkle green- or rainbow-tinted coconut all around base of egg; or use green-paper grass. Scatter Jordan almonds (or jelly beans) here and there in nest. Top egg with nosegay of spring flowers tied with ribbons that fit into your color scheme.

Bûche de Noël

*This fine French masterpiece
is a cherished, chocolate-filled
ceremony at holidaytime*

Bûche de Noël, or Yule Log, is the luscious dessert served in French households on the stroke of midnight each Christmas Eve. It's rich with chocolate, rolled in Chocolate Butter Cream—and we propose it as a sumptuous treat for *any* time of the year.

New Year's Marshmallow Chocolate Cake:

a tall, three-layer dessert, deep in chocolate butter-cream frosting and topped with broiled marshmallows

Coconut-drifted Valentine

This cake—with its pale-pink frosting under a coconut snowfall—was designed to take the center of the stage on such festive occasions as Valentine's Day. The trimmings: sweetheart roses, nestled at its base

87

Easter Song

Grownups admire and children beg —
Cut them all a slice of Easter Egg!

Grand Finale
For an Easter Feast

Day before or ahead of time:

1. Make and bake **four 8″ yellow cake layers** from favorite recipe or a mix. Wrap in **foil,** store overnight. (Or freezer-wrap and freeze; to use, thaw 1 hr. at room temperature.)

2. Make **Posie Cream, p. 177.** Store, covered, overnight, at room temperature.

Early on the day:

1. Cut **cardboard** into egg shape, 12¼″ long; 7¾″ wide at center; 6″ wide at point 1¾″ in from each end; cover with foil. Stir up frosting; tint 2 cups **pale green.**

2. Halve each cake layer crosswise, making two semi-circles. With some white frosting, lightly frost cardboard egg, then one side of a half-layer. Press another half-layer to frosted side; center, upright, with cut edge down, on cardboard. Trim cut edge of other half-layers so two measure 3¾″, two 3½″, two 2¾″ from center of curve to straight edge. Lightly frost one side of each.

3. Place one 3¾″ half-layer on each side of layers on cardboard, joining frosted side to center layers. Join 3½″ layers same way, then 2¾″ layers. With long knife, trim edges, to make cake smooth, oval.

4. Lightly frost egg with pale-green frosting; with rest, refrost entire egg green, retaining its shape. With broad spatulas, lift egg, with cardboard base, to **slightly larger egg-shaped cardboard** or **flat serving dish.**

5. With **toothpick,** lightly draw 7 long curving lines on frosting. With white frosting and **tube no. 16** in **decorating bag,** trace curved lines. With same tube, make each branch by forming a small dot, turning cone slightly, and blending dot into curved line; relax pressure on bag as branch nears long, curving line. Repeat over cake.

6. Move cake to serving table; tuck **galax leaves** under it. With white frosting, and tube **no. 190** in **decorating bag,** drop a row of flowers around cake base. Fill in with more flowers, having a few on leaves. With tweezers, drop **multicolored nonpareils** on each flower, and one on each dot on cake top.

89

May's Prettiest Cake

Early on the day before:

1. Set **colored paper cupcake liners** in twelve 2¾″ cupcake-pan cups. Grease, flour 4¼″ by 2″ round oven-glass baking dish.

2. Make up **1 large pkg. yellow cake mix;** use to fill cupcake cups three fourths full; pour rest into baking dish. Bake cupcakes as label directs; bake larger cake 5 min. longer, or till cake tester inserted in center comes out clean. Cool.

3. Make **May Day Frosting, p. 177.**

4. For maypole, paint a **wooden stick, 10½″ long, ¼″ thick,** with white paint.

Later, day before:

1. Slip each cupcake into **two green paper cupcake liners.**

2. With **red food color,** tint 2 cups frosting light pink. Use to frost tops of cupcakes, edges of liners, top of larger cake.

3. Trace, **on paper,** outline of a tiny philodendron leaf; cut out. Lay on frosted cupcake; then, with **toothpick,** outline leaf; outline 1 or 2 more. Repeat on all cupcakes.

4. With **green food color,** tint ¾ cup frosting soft green. Use in **decorating bag** with **tube no. 4,** to outline and fill in leaves. Outline a big star on larger cake.

5. Make a 1″ white-frosting ball; center on each cupcake. With white frosting **in decorating bag and tube no. 30,** cover each ball with stars, starting at base.

On party day:

1. From **2 yd. each of narrow pale-green, pink,** and **white ribbon,** cut 15″ lengths — 4 of each. Cut **twelve 3″ lengths of cellophane tape,** of same width; use to back one end of each ribbon streamer; then cut taped ends diagonally. Wind rest of green and pink ribbon around maypole; tape in place.

2. Now, ½″ down from top of maypole, arrange untaped ends of streamers, alternating colors and leaving 3″ free at top; secure with tape. Next, loop loose streamer ends; fasten with tape. Tie white ribbon over tape; make bow.

3. Set larger cake on **big, round plate.** With white frosting in **decorating bag** and **tube no. 47,** pipe "ribbon" around bottom of cake. Center maypole; surround with cupcakes. Lay ends of streamers on outside of cupcakes. Set on table.

May Cakes

FAMILY ALBUM

Fill and frost **favorite two-layer cake** with **Snow Peak, p. 178.** Then, with **plain tube for writing no. 4,** and **pink Posie Cream, p. 177,** in **decorating bag,** make stick figures to represent members of the family — even to the dog. Write a message: "With love to Mom."

MAY DAY BASKET

Make and bake **favorite square cake.** Frost sides with **Snow Peak, p. 178.** On cake top, make mound of the frosting — pyramid style — about 2″ high in center and tapering to ⅛″ around top edges of cake.

With rest of frosting, make **impressionistic flowers** on mound. For "**roses,**" use **pink frosting** in **leaf tube no. 68;** make irregular spirals, holding tube at right angle. For **hyacinths,** make cluster of **lavender rosettes** with **rosette tube no. 28;** hold upright and press out. Finish off with **yellow "daisies":** For each, make two X's, as shown, with **plain tube for writing no. 4** held at angle. Add **leaves** with **leaf tube no. 68.** For handle, add **twig,** with **leaves removed.**

MOTHER'S DAY CAKE

Make, bake and cool **angel food cake** from mix as label directs, using square angel food pan. Remove cake from pan; set on **cake plate.** Make up **1 pkg. fluffy white frosting mix;** tint **pale yellow.** Use to frost cake..

Now cut **four 12″ pieces of ribbon.** Make cake resemble package by placing **12″ piece of ribbon** down center of each side, as shown, tucking one end in cake's center hole, other underneath. Make **nosegay of fresh flowers;** tie with **rest of ribbon** in frilly bow. Insert in center of cake.

Birthday Basket for Mother
(pictured on p. 98)

One 9″ or 10″ tube
angel food or
chiffon cake
Cake plate
Snow Peak, p. 178,
tinted pale green
Posie Cream, p. 177

Food colors
Shell tube, no. 30
Decorating bags
Fresh flowers
Paper butterflies
Pipe cleaners

Day before, if desired:

1. Make, bake, cool, wrap, then store cake.

On the day:

1. To make the angel food cake basket shape, cut a half-moon piece of cake (1¾″ at broadest part) from across both the front and back of cake. Then set cake on cake plate, tilting it slightly with some cut cake as prop at back.

2. Make and tint Snow Peak green. Make Posie Cream; tint half pale green, rest a shade darker.

3. Now frost whole cake with pale green Snow Peak. Then, for woven effect, use pale green Posie Cream, and shell tube no. 30, in decorating bag; press out frosting lines all around top and side of cake, keeping lines parallel and about 1″ apart.

4. Next, close to pale green line, press out darker green line. Then weave light and dark green lines up and down, and in and out of first lines.

5. Into center hole insert **small glass,** partly filled with water. In it arrange Mother's favorite flowers in shower effect down side of basket. Add butterflies.

6. For basket handle, tint some pipe cleaners green, others yellow, by placing them in two pie plates, one with **green food color,** other with **yellow food color,** each mixed with **few tablespoons water.** When well soaked, dry on wire cake rack. Then twist into long handle and insert in cake. Tie on **ribbon bow.**

Dad's Checkerboard Cake
(pictured on p. 101)

1 large pkg. yellow-
cake mix
1 large pkg. chocolate-
mint- or chocolate-
cake mix
½ sq. unsweetened
chocolate

28 to 32 blanched
almonds
Butter Cream, p. 175
Double-thick 20″ x 7″
cardboard
Hungarian Chocolate
Frosting, p. 176

Early on day, or day before, if desired:

1. Make up yellow cake mix as label directs. Pour into 15½″ x 4½″ x 4½″ angel cake loaf pan*, bottom of which has been greased and lined with waxed paper. Bake at 350° F. 40 min., or till done. Let cake cool in pan on rack about 1 hr.; remove; finish cooling.

2. Make up, bake, and cool chocolate-mint cake mix in same pan, same way.

3. Wrap cooled cakes in foil.

The day:

1. Melt unsweetened chocolate; into it, dip large end of each almond. Let harden on waxed paper.

2. Make Butter Cream. Slice rounded top from cakes. Halve cakes lengthwise.

3. On cake board or foil-covered, double-thick 20″ by 7″ cardboard, lay four 2″-wide waxed-paper strips in a rectangle. On it, lay one chocolate-cake strip and one yellow-cake strip, slightly apart, with crusts on outside. Frost cut sides between strips with one-fourth of Butter Cream. Press together ·closely; frost top with two-thirds of remaining frosting.

4. Now, on top of these cake strips, set other two strips—chocolate on yellow, yellow on chocolate — with rest of Butter Cream spread between them.

5. Make Hungarian Chocolate Frosting; lightly frost sides and top of cake.

6. Refrost cake with rest of Hungarian Chocolate Frosting. On sides of cake, with small spatula, make stroke marks from base to top edge, leaving a small peak of chocolate at top edge each time.

7. Then, with same spatula, make zig-zag pattern on top of cake, as pictured. Now remove waxed-paper strips.

8. Lay chocolate-tipped almonds around top outer edge of cake, as pictured.

* See p. 181.

Decorating cakes with a "writing tube" is so simple and so speedy that a teen-ager can easily handle it. Suggested point of departure: Have your teen-ager make this cake for Father's Day.

To the Best Dad in All the World

On day before, if desired:

Make, bake, cool, then wrap and store **two Fudge Cake layers, p. 171,** until needed 'on the next day.

On the day:

1. Make **Date Filling, p. 176.** Then make **Dad's Favorite Fudge Frosting, p. 176,** and **Snow Cream, p. 178.**

2. Cut out a **9″ cardboard circle;** cover it with **foil.** Set one of Fudge Cake layers on it. Spread with the Date Filling, then top with the other cake layer. Now frost the top and sides of the cake generously with Dad's Favorite Fudge Frosting.

3. With a **toothpick,** lightly outline tennis racket and message to Dad on cake. (Of course, the tennis racket may be replaced with a baseball glove, golf bag, or any other symbol

of Dad's hobby.) Then, with Snow Cream in **decorating bag,** and **tube no. 2,** make crosswise, then lengthwise "strings" for tennis racket.

4. With Snow Cream in **another decorating bag,** and **tube no. 4,** outline tennis racket. Next, mix **a drop of green food color** with a little Snow Cream; use, **in third decorating bag,** with **tube no. 5,** to fill in tennis racket.

5. Then, with first decorating bag and **tube no. 2,** make straight lines on top of green frosting. With more Snow Cream in **fourth decorating bag,** and **tube no. 5,** write suggested message to Dad, or one of your own.

6. At serving time, place cake on an attractive **cake plate.** Set it in front of Dad's place at the table; then tuck small pieces of **flat fern** around the plate on the table, as a finishing garnish.

Cakes for June

DAD'S TOPPER

Set **favorite filled two-layer cake** on **cardboard circle, 2"** larger, all around, than cake. Frost cardboard brim and cake crown thickly with **white, yellow, or Coffee Posie Cream, p. 177.** Then, with tip of **knife handle,** make markings around brim and crown as shown.

With **rosette tube no. 28** and **Chocolate Posie Cream,** write "Dad" on crown; also make hatband with 2 or 3 touching rows of frosting around hat where it joins brim.

FOR DEPARTING CAMPER

Make **favorite 10" x 5" x 3" loaf cake.** Set cake on **a board** and frost with **Mocha Butter Cream, p. 175.** Then with **Snow Cream, p. 178,** and **plain tube for writing no. 4** in decorating **bag,** write name and address of camper on frosting, make cord and knots. Add **2 chocolate square stamps;** refrigerate.

At party time, take cake from refrigerator and tie a **broad ribbon, stamped with post office stamps,** around board.

DIPLOMA SPECIAL

Frost **favorite filled layer cake** with **chocolate, pale pink, yellow or green Snow Peak, p. 178.**

Just before serving, place daisy chain of **braided fresh daisies** around base of cake.

Also, write congratulatory message on **paper 12" by 8";** roll it up; tie with **ribbon,** then lay on cake top, anchoring with a **pick** if necessary.

94

Monogram Cake

We've yet to meet anyone, young or old, who doesn't love celebrating a birthday with a wonderful, fanciful birthday cake—the kind that's so pretty you almost hate to cut it. This one is just such a cake.

1 large pkg. white-cake mix	20 black-eyed Susans
Posie Cream, p. 177	Variegated ivy
Large, oblong black tray, 21½" by 13½"	Philodendron leaves
	Yellow birthday candles, 3" long

Early on the day:

1. Make up, then bake cake batter in two greased 8" x 8" x 2" cake pans at 350° F. about 30 min., or until done.

2. While cakes cool make Posie Cream.

3. On **7" square of paper or cardboard**, draw one of the birthday child's initials; cut out pattern. Repeat with other initial.

4. Lay pattern for first initial on top of one of cake squares. With sharp knife, carefully cut around pattern, through to bottom of cake; remove excess cake. Using second cake square, cut out second initial same way. (If you prefer three initials in your Monogram Cake, bake three cake squares and cut three paper patterns and three cake initials.)

5. Carefully brush loose crumbs from cakes. With **eight 12" by 3" strips of waxed paper,** cover area of oblong serving tray where initials are to be placed. Lay cake initials, side by side, on these waxed paper strips.

6. To set crumbs, lightly frost all cake surfaces with some of Posie Cream. With rest of it generously frost cakes. Carefully pull out paper strips.

7. Arrange black-eyed Susans around cake initials, as pictured. Tuck ivy and philodendron here and there. Insert yellow candles in initials.

At serving time:

Arrange cake where refreshments are to be served. Ours was on a pale-yellow organdy cloth, and with it we served punch. You might prefer hot or iced tea or coffee.

Cakes for July

OLD GLORY

A wonderful cake for a Fourth of July picnic. Bake **favorite cake** in 12″ x 8″ x 2″ pan; then frost it right in pan for easy totin'.

Spread a rectangle of **light blue frosting** in upper left hand corner as base for stars. With **leaf tube no. 68** and **pink frosting**, make stripe along top, then bottom, then center of cake. Now place two more between top and center, and between bottom and center. Retrace if stripes should be thicker.

Now, using **white frosting,** fill in white stripes as shown. Then switch to **rosette tube no. 28,** and press out stars on the blue field.

FIRECRACKERS, BANG! BANG!

Buy **3 jelly rolls 6″ by 4″,** or roll your own. Spread outside of rolls with **jelly**; roll in **grated coconut**. With a little **blue Posie Cream, p. 177,** in **plain writing tube no. 4,** write "July" on one firecracker, "the" on second, and "4th" on third. Set on **dark blue or silver platter.** For fuse insert **3″ piece of heavy twine** in top of each.

THE BIRTHDAY CHILD

Frost **jelly-filled layer cake** with stiffly beaten **Snow Peak, p. 178.** Use **rosette tube no. 28,** and **decorating bag** filled with **light blue Snow Peak** to make pinwheels or spirals around sides and on top of cake. Insert **short, fat red candles** in center of pinwheels on top of cake. If you wish, encircle each large candle with the usual small birthday candles (either white or light blue) if the birthday child is over five and less than 21.

To Mother With Love

Preliminaries:

Get out **one 8″ layer-cake pan** plus a **3″ cupcake cup pan.** Cut **10″ cardboard circle.** Use **straw or plastic hatstand with flat top,** or **plastic hatbox of suitable size.**

Cake for hat:

Prepare, bake, then cool **1 large pkg. favorite cake mix** as label directs, filling one 8″ layer cake pan half full, and making cupcakes from rest of batter. Cool in pans on wire rack 10 to 15 min. Remove from pans; then cool on rack. Use cake layer for hat, cupcakes for family dessert next day.

When cool, place **7″ paper circle** on top of 8″ cake. With sharp knife, cut straight up and down all the way around. Remove paper circle; lift out layer of cake. Brush loose crumbs from layer. Then proceed as follows.

Trimming hat

Make up **Orange Butter Cream, p. 177.** Use a little to "glue" 7″ cake (crown) onto **10″ cardboard circle (brim),** placing crown so it is 1″ in from edge of brim in back.

Frost crown and brim, saving small amount of frosting for ribbon. Refrigerate hat 30 min. Then make straw by drawing **4-tined fork** through frosting, in pattern pictured.

Ribbon: Using **red** and **blue food colors,** tint leftover frosting purple. Put in **decorating bag** with **leaf tube no. 68.** Starting at back of hat, at base of crown, press out continuous ribbon around hat crown; neatly overlap ends. Now, starting at back of hat, close to top edge of crown, make second row of ribbon. Around base of crown, arrange **fresh cherries on stems, strawberries, raspberries, and a few tiny blossoms.** Tuck in a **few small leaves.**

The Presentation

Balance hat on hatstand as shown. (Or place hat in plastic hatbox; tie with pretty ribbon.) Arrange **gifts for Mother** around base (or on top of and beside hatbox).

When you bake with love for a leaven,
You may get a cake straight out of heaven . . .
A cake that's a sonnet, a cake that's a bonnet!

Birthday Basket for Mother

Surprise for Mother

½ gal. strawberry ice
   cream
1 qt. vanilla ice cream
2 cups heavy cream,
   whipped

Red food color
1 4-oz. box large
   marshmallows
Granulated sugar
5 candles in holders

Several days ahead:

1. Use strawberry ice cream to fill center of **9" torte-and-cake pan** (with flat insert in place); fill rest of pan with vanilla ice cream. Press down to form smooth surface. Place in freezer until **firm.**

2. Remove sides from torte pan, leaving "cake" on pan insert. Immediately frost top and sides of cake with two thirds of whipped cream. With a few drops of red food color tint rest of whipped cream pink; use with **no. 5 tube** in **decorating bag** to make lattice on top of cake. Freeze until needed.

3. Meanwhile, with scissors, snip each marshmallow into 5 pieces. With fingers, stretch each piece into a petal. Arrange 5 large petals, overlapping them, in tiny circle; press together. Insert 5 small petals in center, overlapping them and pressing petals together to form blossom. Allow 5 blossoms for top of cake, rest of petals for base. Sprinkle blossoms and petals with granulated sugar tinted red with a few drops of red food color. Freeze until needed.

About 15 min. before serving:

1. Remove cake from freezer. Place, still on pan insert, on serving plate. Place blossoms on top; arrange petals around base; insert candles. Make 16 servings.

P.S. This is an ideal cake for the busy woman. She can make it ahead at her leisure, and not worry about it until 15 min. before serving.

Celebrating Dad's Day

13" x 9" x 2" chocolate
  cake
Cardboard
Foil
Twice recipe Flower
  Cream, p. 176
Food colors
Cocoa

Chocolate kisses
Tissue paper
Square thin chocolate-
  peppermint patties
Enclosure card
Gold-paper crown
Gold ribbon

1. Trim cake to straighten edges; set on **13" by 9" piece of cardboard.** From more cardboard cut out cuffs and tie; cover with foil. Frost cuffs with Flower Cream. Now cut **6" cardboard circle,** removing pie-shaped wedge 2" long and 2" wide at outer edge; cover with foil. Next cut **12" by 1½" cardboard strip;** staple ends together to form ring.

2. For collar, center ring (neckband) on 6" circle. Heap some of frosting around and up to top of neckband; with spatula, smooth into collar shape shown. Frost inside of neckband.

3. Tint ½ cup of remaining frosting yellow; reserve. Tint rest of frosting blue; use to frost both cake and foil center of collar. Set finished collar and cuffs in place on cake.

4. To rest of blue frosting, add enough cocoa to tint brown; use to frost tie, with generous knot. Using **no. 19 tube** in **decorating bag** and yellow frosting, make stripes on tie, slanting those at lower part in one direction, and those on knot in opposite direction. With wet spatula, smooth stripes; then, with tip of knife, trim sides of tie for clear-cut line. Set tie on cake, propping knot with small ball of foil.

5. Cut tips from chocolate kisses; then arrange kisses, bottom side up, as cuff links. Make a tiny ball of foil, and add to tie as stickpin. On tissue paper in center of table, set cake. Just before partytime, press mints into sides of cake, all the way around, to form box. Add enclosure card; adjust crown and ribbon.

Dad's Checkerboard Cake— which looks complicated but isn't. (A chocolate cake and a yellow cake are halved lengthwise and put together with frosting)

SUSAN'S PETAL CAKE

1 pkg. angel- or chiffon-cake mix
3 pt. favorite ice creams
1 pkg. fluffy-white-frosting mix
Liquid green food color
Fruits and walnuts

1 In a 3-qt. ovenproof mixing bowl. Susan makes up the cake mix as label directs (hers is lemon-custard angel-cake mix). Then she bakes cake in same bowl at 350°F. 45 min., or till done. To cool cake, she inverts bowl with edges resting on two inverted cake pans. Then, with long spatula, she carefully loosens cake on all sides, removes it from bowl, cools it on rack.

2 While her bowl cake cools, Susan uses a no. 16 scoop to make up 12 ice-cream balls from three or more favorite flavors (Susan used chocolate, coffee, pistachio, and strawberry ice creams). She stores these on a cookie sheet in the freezer. Now, with a sharp knife at an angle and starting 1" in from top edge of cake, she cuts down and then around cake, then removes the shallow, cone-shape cake piece thus formed. Last, she brushes all loose crumbs from the cake.

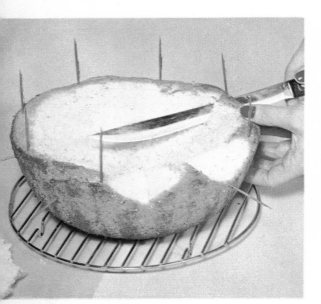

3 Now, around top cake edge, Susan places eight toothpicks, 3½" apart and at right angle to edge. Between every two picks and 1" below, she centers a pick. Starting with one of picks at top edge, she makes a diagonal cut down to lower pick, then a cut from next pick at top edge down to same lower pick. She removes wedge to make one petal. She makes seven more.

4 Susan makes up frosting mix as label directs, tints it pale green. She inverts cake on inverted bowl, lightly frosts it to set crumbs. With rest of frosting and small spatula, she makes three stroke marks on each petal. At dessert time, she sets cake, right side up, on stand, fills it with ice-cream balls, then garnishes it with favorite fruits and walnuts. For each serving, she lifts ice-cream balls from one of petals to dessert plate, then cuts out petal to set beside them. ◆

102

Our teen-age cook's triumphant dessert, heaped high with ice-cream balls

For a Sweet Girl Graduate

4 favorite 9″ cake
  layers
Three 4½″- and one
  12″-cardboard circles
Twice recipe for
  Snow Peak, p. 178

Yellow food color
¾ cup flaked coconut
½ sq. unsweetened
  chocolate, shaved
Foil or saran
Cedar branches

Day before if desired:

Make, bake, then cool cake layers; store, covered.

On party day:

1. Set aside 1 cake layer. Then set each of remaining cake layers on 4½″ cardboard circle; with sharp knife, cut nine or ten 1½″-deep V-shaped pieces from each, making daisy shape.

2. **For white daisy:** Frost 1 "daisy" cake white; with tablespoon or spatula, drop big mound of frosting on each petal, leaving well in center. **For pale-yellow daisy:** Tint rest of frosting delicate yellow; use to frost daisy cake as before. **For deep-yellow daisy:** Add more yellow color to rest of frosting; frost daisy cake as before.

3. To coconut, add bit of yellow color; toss until evenly tinted; pile half of it in center of white daisy. To rest of coconut, add a few more drops of yellow color; toss; pile in center of pale-yellow daisy. Smooth edges of well in center of deep-yellow daisy; pile chocolate in center.

4. Now cover 12″ cardboard circle with foil. On it, set pale-yellow daisy, with deep-yellow daisy close by as shown. Then, using 6″ cake round (cut from reserved layer) as prop, arrange white daisy so it overlaps the other two. Tuck in cedar branches.

Memory Book Cake

Day before:

Cakes: With **2 large pkg. yellow-cake mix,** make, then bake, two cakes, one after the other, in a greased, well-floured 13″ x 9″ x 2″ baking pan, at 350° F. about 40 min., or until done. Cool; remove from pan; wrap in **foil.**

Gumdrop roses: Have ready **4 doz. small pink gumdrops.** With rolling pin, on wooden board, flatten four gumdrops one at a time. Cut small piece from one end of one flattened gumdrop; tightly roll up this piece to form center of rose. Attach to center, by pinching, one at a time, other three flattened gumdrops, overlapping to resemble petals of rose. Gently bend back petals to shape rose. Refrigerate. Make eight more roses.

Gumdrop buds: Flatten one gumdrop; fold two short edges together, without creasing; pinch bottom edges together. Refrigerate. Make two more buds.

Early day of party:

1. With **sheet of dark-red foil,** cover top of **16½″ by 13″ cardboard oblong,** taping overlap to underside. Set unwrapped cakes on foil so two long sides meet.

2. With ruler, measure 1″ in from all outside cake edges; mark with **toothpicks.** With a **long sharp knife,** and picks as guide, cut off wedge-shaped pieces to cake bottom; remove wedges and picks.

3. Now, on each page, with picks, make lengthwise mark, 1″ from center "binding." Then cut on angle toward center to within ½″ of cake bottom. Lift out each strip, and lay along cut center edge; with hands, flatten to give a curved effect to page.

4. Make twice Posie Cream, p. 177.

5. To set crumbs, lightly frost all book surfaces. Reserving 1 cup of remaining frosting, use rest to frost book generously, keeping curved effect of pages. Then dip spatula in very hot water and smooth the frosting.

6. With 4-tined fork, mark sides to resemble pages, as pictured. Wipe foil edges clean.

7. With **green food color,** tint ½ cup reserved frosting green; put in **decorating bag** with **tube no. 5.** Add ½ sq. **unsweetened chocolate, melted,** to rest of frosting; put in second **decorating bag** with **tube no. 4.**

8. With toothpick, in soft frosting, on left page lightly write words "Memory Book Cake." Then, with chocolate frosting in **decorating bag,** cover letters; also fill in opening at both ends of center "binding" (see picture.)

9. Arrange gumdrop roses, buds on book pages, as shown. Split **8 small green gumdrop leaves;** set in place. With green frosting in decorating bag, make stems joining roses, leaves.

Near partytime:

Arrange Memory Book Cake as centerpiece; tuck fresh rose leaves under corners.

105

New Tricks With Treats

(pictured on p. 113)

Several days ahead, make cupcakes:

KENTUCKY CUPCAKES

2 sq. unsweetened chocolate	¾ cup buttermilk
1 teasp. allspice	2 tablesp. any fruit juice
¼ teasp. cinnamon	½ cup seedless black raspberry preserves
1½ teasp. baking soda	
1½ cups sifted all-purpose flour	½ cup light or dark raisins
⅓ cup shortening	½ cup currants
½ cup granulated sugar	½ cup chopped walnuts
½ cup brown sugar, firmly packed	1 pkg. fluffy white frosting mix
2 eggs, separated	Yellow food color
	Uncooked dried prunes

1. Start heating oven to 350° F. Line sixteen 3″ cupcake-pan cups with paper liners you buy.

2. Melt unsweetened chocolate over **hot, not boiling, water,** and cool. Sift together allspice, cinnamon, baking soda, and all-purpose flour.

3. In large bowl, with mixer at medium speed, mix shortening with granulated and brown sugars, then with egg yolks, until **very light and fluffy**—about 4 min. altogether.

4. Combine buttermilk and fruit juice. At low speed, add these to egg-yolk mixture, alternately with flour mixture, beginning and ending with flour mixture; beat **just until smooth.**

5. Add seedless black raspberry preserves and cooled melted unsweetened chocolate; blend thoroughly.

6. Fold in raisins, currants, and walnuts. Beat egg whites until stiff, but not dry. Fold into batter; pour into prepared cupcake-pan cups.

7. Bake cupcakes 25 to 30 min., or until they spring back when lightly touched with finger. Remove from pans and cool on cake racks.

8. Store cupcakes, wrapped in foil, in refrigerator.

On the day, complete cupcakes as follows:

1. Make up the fluffy white frosting mix as label directs. With yellow food color, tint it yellow. Use to swirl on top of cupcakes.

2. From uncooked dried prune snip a long narrow piece of prune. With your fingers, shape it into a curved, mouthlike piece. Set piece of prune in place on top of one of cupcakes as a mouth.

3. Now cut two small circles from a prune; set in place as eyes. Cut one small circle from a prune; set in place as nose.

4. Repeat with more prunes, until all cupcakes are done. Makes 16.

Serve cupcakes with cocoa, tea, or coffee.

Or, do try serving them with these fascinating Halloween Faces, which are sure to delight your guests:

HALLOWEEN FACES

Early in day or day before:

1. Make up **1 pkg. apple-flavored gelatin** as package label directs; set aside, not in refrigerator.

2. Drain **one 1-lb. 13-oz. can cling peach halves.** Place one peach half, rounded side up, in bottom of each sherbet glass or nappy dish, as pictured.

3. On each peach half, make a face, using **pieces of uncooked dried prunes** as features, and poking each one into place with a **toothpick.**

4. Use **a strip of citron or angelica** for pumpkin stem, inserting it at the center top of the peach.

5. Then pour the cooled, but still liquid, apple flavored gelatin over the peach faces, covering each one completely in the sherbet glass.

6. Refrigerate faces until set. Then serve with the Halloween cupcakes to little folks, teenagers, and grownups alike. All will vote Halloween was never so special before. Makes 7 to 9 servings.

It's Halloween

MR. JACK O' LANTERN

Make one and one-half times recipe for **Snow Peak, p. 178.** Frost a **filled 9″ three-layered cake** generously with it. Then place spoonfuls of frosting around outer edge of top layer. With spatula build top half of sides of cake with more frosting to look like a pumpkin. Cut a **piece of candied citron** about 2″ high to resemble a stem. Use **grated unsweetened chocolate** for eyes, nose, and mouth, by picking up a pinch with thumb, index finger and middle finger, and then touching frosting with it for eyes, nose, mouth.

OCTOBER TRIO

Frost **three 8″ x 8″ x 2″ cakes** with **Snow Peak, p. 178, tinted yellow.** With **toothpick** trace outline of bat on first cake, pumpkin on second, and black cat on third. Melt **½ cup semisweet chocolate pieces** over **hot, not boiling water.** Stir in **¼ cup white corn syrup;** cool slightly. Pour slowly around inside edge of outline of cat and bat; then fill in center, spreading with spatula if necessary. Stir **orange marmalade** till "runny"; use to fill in pumpkin. With **grated unsweetened chocolate** make eyes, nose, and mouth on it. Sprinkle some chocolate, too, on cat and bat. Set cakes side by side on tray. Nice as centerpiece.

BEWITCHED

Beg, borrow or steal **an ice cream cone.** Frost it and a **3″ cookie** with chocolate coating (melt **2 sq. unsweetened chocolate** with **1 teasp. butter;** cool). Place on top of **orange-frosted cake** to resemble witch's hat. Around bottom edge of cake, place border of **Halloween shaped candies** — pumpkins, owls, witches.

Celebration Orange-Chiffon Cake

(pictured on p. 114)

This lofty orange chiffon cake is designed to feast the eye as well as the palate—and incidentally, to win the hostess new laurels. It's breath-taking as a birthday bow, whether the honored one be a grown-up or one of your youngsters.

5 medium-egg yolks, unbeaten
1 cup egg whites (7 or 8 medium eggs)
2¼ cups sifted cake flour
1½ cups granulated sugar
3 teasp. double-acting baking powder
1 teasp. salt
½ cup salad oil
3 tablesp. grated orange rind
¾ cup orange juice
½ teasp. cream of tartar
3 or 4 oranges
2 pkg. fluffy-white-frosting mix

On the day before:

1. About one hour ahead, set out unbeaten egg yolks, also egg whites.

2. When ready to make chiffon cake, start heating oven to 325° F. Into large bowl, sift cake flour, granulated sugar, baking powder, and salt.

3. Make well in flour mixture; pour salad oil into it. Add unbeaten egg yolks, orange rind, and orange juice. With mixer at medium speed, beat mixture till nice and smooth.

4. Measure egg whites into another large bowl; add cream of tartar. Beat egg whites till they hold **very stiff peaks. (Do not underbeat egg whites,** for they should be stiffer than for an angel-food cake or pie meringue.)

5. Slowly pour egg-yolk mixture over beaten egg whites, folding them in gently with rubber spatula or spoon. **Do not stir them in.** Continue folding over and over until yolk mixture is just blended with egg whites, but no more.

6. Now carefully turn orange cake batter into **ungreased** 4"-deep 10" angel tube pan. With rubber spatula, cut through batter in pan two or three times, so that you level the batter from top to bottom and thus prevent large holes in the finished chiffon cake.

7. Bake chiffon cake at 325° F. 55 min., then at 350° F. 10 to 15 min., or until cake tester inserted in center comes out clean.

8. Now invert cake, resting it on center tube of pan, on side "ears", or on the neck of a bottle; let hang in pan 1 hr. or until cold. Then turn right side up, insert spatula between cake and side of pan until tip touches bottom. Then press gently against side of pan, cutting away clinging cake. Pull spatula out; repeat all around edge and tube. Then invert cake on cake rack and lift off pan. Store until next day.

On next day:

1. Cover top outer area of **an attractive cake plate** with **four 2"-wide waxed-paper strips** in a square. Center inverted chiffon cake on these strips.

2. With a sharp knife, cut the top and bottom from each orange; then slice the center portion into even slices, ¼" thick. Now halve each orange slice, as pictured, then set aside till later.

3. Make up frosting mix as label directs. Lightly frost cake to set crumbs; then generously refrost it.

Now, starting at base of cake and working up to top center edge, use a 1¼"-wide spatula to make diagonal marks in frosting that end in peaks at center top of cake.

4. Next, remove waxed paper strips; then press the halved orange slices into the frosting around the base of the cake in the neat even row pictured.

5. Now the cake is ready to arrange as a centerpiece wherever the birthday child's party is to be. **One large lighted candle** may grace the top of it, if you like.

Quick Celebration Cake:

Make up **1 pkg. orange-chiffon-cake mix** as label directs. Fold **3 tablesp. grated orange rind** into batter. Turn into 4"-deep 10" tube pan; then bake and cool as label directs.

When cake is cool, remove from pan. Make up **1 pkg. fluffy-white-frosting mix.** Use as in steps 1, 2, 3, and 4, under "On next day:", above.

108

Pet Quartette

(pictured on p. 115)

For each of the pets in our quartette you will need:

1 cast aluminum lamb mold, 12½″ by 7½″	Lamb Mold Cake, p. 172 Foil Cardboard

1. Grease and flour entire mold **well**. Make Lamb Mold Cake as directed.

2. Into part of mold showing lamb's face, pour cake batter; level off with spatula, cover with other part of mold. Carefully set in 350° F. oven, in same position; bake 1 hr., or until done.

3. Cool cake in mold 5 min.; then gently loosen edges with spatula; carefully turn onto cake rack, in natural position; finish cooling.

4. On foil-covered cardboard, cut slightly larger than base of cake, set lamb cake in natural position; then transform into a pet below.

Holiday Stag:

Make **1 batch Butter Cream, p. 175.** Reserving 2 tablesp., use rest to frost lamb cake. Over his back and head, sprinkle **silver dragées.** From **white pipe cleaners,** make antlers; gently press into position as shown. Tint 1 tablesp. reserved frosting green; apply with **toothpick** for stag's eyes; add **snipped, tiny gumdrop pupils.** Tint rest of frosting pink; apply with toothpick for nose.

Around stag's neck, tie **red ribbon** with **small bell** and **holly berries** attached. Into frosting around neck, press **holly leaves.** Lay more **holly leaves** around base of stag; then tuck **colorful Christmas balls** here and there.

Fawn for Easter:

From **heavy paper,** make 2 tiny horns. Make **1 batch Mocha Butter Cream, p. 175.** Use to frost lamb cake and horns; set horns in place as shown. On back of fawn, arrange **semisweet-chocolate pieces** and **snipped tiny marshmallows** as shown. For nose, press **half a tiny black gumdrop** in place (save gumdrop piece for pupils).

Mix **1 tablesp. confectioners' sugar** with **a little milk.** Tint some **green;** apply with toothpick for eyes; halve **reserved gumdrop** for pu-

pils. Use remaining frosting and toothpick to frost inside of ears. On fawn's head, sprinkle **a bit of shaved chocolate.** Into frosting around fawn's neck press **daisies;** arrange more daisies and leaves around base.

To **3 or 4 twigs,** with **cellophane tape,** attach **a few Jordan almonds.** Set in **ball of modeling clay** behind fawn.

Puss in Basket:

Cut ears from lamb cake; with toothpicks, fasten them higher on head. Make **1 batch Butter Cream,** p. 175. Reserve 2 tablesp.; to rest, add **1 cup flaked coconut;** use to fill out cheeks and frost puss. Tint 1 tablesp. reserved frosting green; apply with toothpick for eyes, adding bits of **black gumdrops** for pupils. Tint remaining frosting pink; apply with toothpick for nose and mouth. Add **toothpick whiskers.**

For hat, pierce **blossoms of violets** with **short toothpicks;** press into head; at back of head, fasten **2 narrow violet ribbons;** tie ends under chin. Move puss into **basket lined with red and white shredded cellophane;** add **bow.**

Pup on Pillow:

Make **lamb cake.** Also make **13″ x 9″ x 2″ cake** from **1 large pkg. cake mix;** cool. Place each on **foil-covered cardboard,** cut to fit. Cut ears from lamb cake, keeping shape of head. Make **2 batches Butter Cream, p. 175.** To ½ cup, add **1 sq. unsweetened chocolate, melted;** tint ⅓ cup **pink;** tint ⅔ cup **blue;** reserve all. Use rest of Butter Cream to frost pillow, then puppy; with **fork,** rough up puppy's coat.

From **bakers' pound cake,** cut ears 2½″ x 1½″ x ¼″; frost with **chocolate frosting;** with **toothpicks,** attach to head. With chocolate frosting, make eyes, then 2 spots; with tip of **toothpick** and some of pink frosting, make tongue. Make nose with a **snipped black gumdrop.** To **narrow ribbon,** attach **gold paper heart;** tie around pup's neck.

For alternate stripes and binding on pillow, use **blue frosting** with **tube no. 47,** and **pink frosting** with **tube no. 45.**

Now place puppy on pillow. Into pillow, press stems of **1 pink** and **1 yellow carnation** and **leaves** as shown.

Santa's Cake

(pictured on p. 116)

To make our Santa's Cake you'll need the following items. Read all directions carefully, while referring to figures 1 and 2 and picture.

2 egg whites	Round toothpicks
3 cups confectioners' sugar	1 6½-oz. pkg. miniature marshmallows
Red and blue paste food colors	Silver dragées
4 sugar (not waffle) ice-cream cones	7 or 8 large marshmallows
2 large waffle-cone cuplets	Santa's Tree, below
Red sugar sprinkles	Santa's Sack, below
	A favorite frosted cake

Few days ahead of serving:

1. Make this Ornamental Icing:

In large bowl, with mixer at medium speed, beat egg whites with confectioners' sugar 15 min., or till very stiff. In second bowl, with red food color, tint half of icing bright red. Cover both bowls with damp cloths.

2. Make Santa's Arms:

On one of sugar ice-cream cones make mark 2" from point; gently cut off at mark all around. Repeat with second cone.

3. Make Santa's Legs:

On third sugar ice-cream cone make mark 2½" from its point; gently cut it off at this mark all around. Repeat with fourth cone.

4. Make Santa's Body:

For body, spread red icing around top of one inverted waffle-cone cuplet; insert it in second one. With red icing, thinly frost it; then frost arms, legs; roll in sprinkles.

Fill arm and leg cones with red icing. Attach them with toothpicks inserted part way into body. Sprinkle joinings with red sprinkles.

5. Make Santa's Fur Trim:

Halve 10 miniature marshmallows horizontally; frost cut sides with white icing; stick around lower edge of top cone cuplet. Attach 3 silver dragées as buttons.

6. Make Santa's Head:

Halve a large marshmallow horizontally. On top of one half, glue, with white icing, a whole large marshmallow. Now cut 2 thin strips of marshmallow, ½" long, for brows; one thin strip of marshmallow, 1¼" long, for mustache. Shape each with fingers, twirling ends to point.

With dab of red icing, tint pink 1 tablesp. white icing. Frost one silver dragée for nose; front side of upper marshmallow for face. Immediately press brows, nose, mustache in place.

Frost flat top of body with white icing. Insert toothpick through its center; fasten head to other end. With toothpick as brush, and blue color, paint in eyes; use red for mouth.

7. Make Santa's Beard:

Slice 15 miniature marshmallows in half horizontally. With white icing, attach them, in 3 overlapping rows, to face to build up beard.

8. Make Santa's Hair:

Attach whole miniature marshmallows, side by side, to back of head.

9. Make Santa's Hat (fig. 2)

Split a large marshmallow up to center top; open it, lay cut side down, then cut one end to a point. Frost with red icing; roll in red sprinkles. Frost top of head with red icing;

attach hat. Place a half toothpick under tip end of hat to hold it away from head, at a jaunty angle, until set. Cut two long pieces from large marshmallow for fur trim; attach with icing. Roll a bit of marshmallow into ball; attach with icing to end of cap.

10. Make Santa's Mittens:

Flatten a miniature marshmallow between fingers; with scissors, snip out a small V, for mitten shape; repeat.

11. Make Santa's Cuffs:

Cut 2 long strips from large marshmallows; trim to desired length.

12. Make Santa's Boots:

Cut a large marshmallow in half horizontally; trim sides of each half to make foot-shaped boot. Make boot cuffs as for cuffs above.

13. Attach Santa's Mittens, Boots, Cuffs:

With white icing attach mittens to arms. Spread inside of two cuffs with white icing; use to encircle wrists. Repeat when attaching boots, cuffs to legs.

14. Make Santa's Tree. You'll need:

8 pointed waxed-paper cups, at least 5″ high	**12″ piece of wire**
Chartreuse, blue, and green poster paint	**1 striped cellophane straw**

Trim cups (buy at soda fountain) to these heights: 1½″, 2″, 2½″, 3″, 3½″, 4″, 4½″, 5″. Notch open end of each.

Now, to chartreuse paint, add some detergent powder to make it stick to cups; repeat with dark green, then blue paint. Paint cups, alternating colors.

Next, for tree trunk, insert wire (wire from coat hanger will do) into striped straw. (Or use painted, striped wooden dowel as trunk.)

Then assemble tree (see picture):

Skewer tallest cup onto tree trunk, so it rests one-third the way down. Put on rest of cups in order of height. With icing, attach tinted miniature marshmallows, candies, dragées.

15. Next make Santa's Sack:

Cut piece of red cloth 7½″ by 3″. Fold in half, stitch a seam on either side, then turn inside out. Fill with candies.

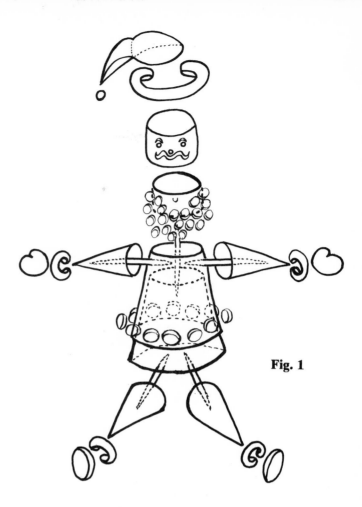

Fig. 1

Day before serving:

Make and bake your favorite layer or oblong cake. (For ours, we filled a 7″-by-2½″-cake pan and a 10″-by-2½″-cake pan half full of batter from 2 pkg. yellow-cake mix. They baked at 350° F. — 45 min. for 7″ pan; 50 to 60 min. for 10″ pan.) Store.

Early on day to be served:

Make up your favorite fluffy white frosting (or use 2 pkg. frosting mix), then use to fill and frost cake. On center top place an inch mound of leftover white Ornamental Icing.

Let icing set a little, then **firmly** plant Santa's tree, slightly tilted to right, in top of cake. Then set Santa **securely** down in icing mound, so his left hand seems to hold the tree, and his feet hang slightly over edge. Put sack at his side.

Decorate cake as pictured, using silver dragées (put on with tweezers) to form arches over red-and-white peppermint candies. Use candy-mint leaves around tops of layers.

To cut cake, remove Santa tree, and sack.

Fig. 2

111

Santa's Socks

Day before:

Start heating oven to 350° F. Grease bottom of **17″-x-11½″-x-2″ roasting pan.** Make up **2 large pkg. favorite cake mix** as label directs, turning batter, as made, into roasting pan. Bake 1 hr. 10 min., or until done. Cool in pan on rack; remove.

Meanwhile, make up twice recipe for **Posie Cream,** p. 177. With **red food color,** tint ½ cup red; with **blue and green food colors,** tint ½ cup dark green; with **yellow food color,** tint ½ cup pale yellow.

On **waxed paper,** trace, then cut out sock pattern; lay on one long side of cake; cut out cake sock. From opposite long side, cut second cake sock. Also cut out 2 **cardboard socks;** cover with **foil;** top each with cake sock.

With white frosting, lightly frost each sock; frost again. With spatula, on top and side, draw diagonal lines for knitted effect. With green frosting in **decorating bag** and **tube no. 4,** make trees, birds. With white frosting in **decorating bag** and **tube no. 46,** make 1¼″ border of close ribbing at top.

With red frosting in **decorating bag** and **tube no. 4,** make candles, canes, horns, name. With yellow frosting in **decorating bag** and **tube no. 2,** make stars; scatter **silver dragées** here and there. Attach **red ribbon bow** to top corner of each sock. Refrigerate.

Before dinnertime:

Arrange cake-socks, side by side, in center of table, with **greens** here and there. Makes 24 servings.

112

NEW TRICKS WITH TREATS

For a Halloween party, or for the Halloween hobgoblins who knock on your front door, we present these extra-delicious cupcakes with frosting funny faces. And another idea for dessert on the night of October 31: pumpkin faces made of peaches, chilled under a shining glaze of gelatin.

Celebration Orange Chiffon Cake

Pet Quartette

Our Santa's Cake

Shower, Wedding and Anniversary Cakes   V

Shower Special

(pictured on p. 125)

White bond paper
Green food color
1 empty 1 lb. 13-oz. can
1 batch Ornamental
    Frosting, p. 177
5 homemade or bakers'
    6″ cake layers

Cardboard circle, 6″ across
Foil
Wooden skewer
Decorating tube no. 27
Decorating bags

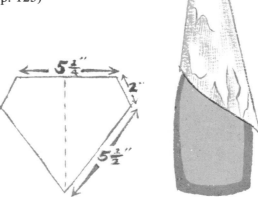

Day before:

1. For 2 handles on watering can, cut 2 strips from white bond paper, each 8½″ by 2″; round off ends slightly. With green food color, tint Ornamental Frosting light green; use to frost one side of each paper strip.

2. Then lay paper strips, frosting side up, over the empty can (it's 4″ in diameter) turned on its side, until frosting is dry. (Can won't roll if a bit of crumpled paper is tucked under one end).

3. For spout, cut white bond paper in the shape and dimensions shown above, having it 6″ across at widest part. Tape 2″ sides together, having them overlap ½″.

4. Frost spout green; place over soft-drink bottle as shown, so frosting dries.

5. With damp cloth, cover bowl of remaining frosting; refrigerate.

On party day:

1. With green frosting, fill the 5 cake layers, stacking one on another. Cover 6″ cardboard circle with foil; set filled cake layers on it; then frost all over.

2. About 1″ down from top of cake, insert wooden skewer part way; from it, hang spout; press end of spout into cake to secure.

3. Carefully frost insides of handles; then press ends of one handle crosswise into top of cake; press ends of other handle into side of cake opposite spout, as pictured.

4. Tint about ½ cup green Ornamental Frosting a deeper green; spread on cake top under handle to represent opening in can. Also, carefully spread some of deeper green Ornamental Frosting inside the tip of the spout.

5. With rest of Ornamental Frosting and tube no. 27 in decorating bag, decorate handles and spout of watering can with the ribbon design shown; add a strip of the same at the bottom. With same tube, make rosettes around the sides as shown.

6. Set watering can in place on party table; surround it with a few pansies and one or two small garden tools as we did.

P.S. Needless to say, your Shower Special can match any favorite color scheme.

Garden tools may be omitted, and any flowers may be used.

It's also a nice centerpiece for a garden-club luncheon, a gardening addict's birthday, or a springtime party.

117

Window Garden

(pictured on p. 125)

1 batch Ornamental
   Frosting, p. 177
Salad oil
4 mixing bowls
Food colors
Decorating bags
Decorating tubes,
   no. 115, 47, 193
Long-loaf angel cake
   pan (15½" x 4½" x
   4½")
2 large pkg. yellow-
   cake mix

Cardboard oblong,
   12" by 4½"
Foil
1 batch Butter Cream,
   p. 175
2 sq. unsweetened
   chocolate, melted
Bottled chocolate
   sprinkles
5 4½" wooden skewers
18 large marshmallows
5 toothpicks

Several days ahead, make leaves as follows:

1. Make one batch of Ornamental Frosting.

2. Invert, then generously oil sides of the mixing bowls.

3. With green food color, tint about one third of Ornamental Frosting pale green; place in decorating bag with tube no. 115. (Reserve rest of frosting).

4. Starting at bottom of one of bowls, press out frosting up and over bowl side, pulling up tube near top to make pointed tip of leaf. Repeat, making about 3 dozen leaves in all to allow for breakage, etc.

5. Let leaves stand overnight, or until dry. Next morning CAREFULLY lift them off bowls and lay, on curved sides, on waxed-paper lined tray; dry at least 12 hr.

Day before, make window box, as follows:

1. Start heating oven to 375° F.

2. Grease and flour the long-loaf angel-cake pan.

3. Make up the two yellow cake mixes, one after the other, as label directs, pouring both batters into the pan.

4. Bake the cake 1 hr. 15 min., or until a cake tester inserted in center comes out clean. Cool 10 min., remove from pan and complete cooling.

5. Trim top of cake level. Then, on bottom of cooled cake, 2" in from both ends, make a diagonal cut to top of cake; remove these wedges.

6. Cover cardboard oblong with foil. Place cake on it as window box.

7. Now make Butter Cream, p. 175. Then tint ⅓ cup Butter Cream pale green with food color; reserve. Into ¾ cup Butter Cream gradually stir melted unsweetened chocolate; use to frost top of cake smoothly.

8. Then, over chocolate surface, generously shake enough bottled chocolate sprinkles to cover the chocolate frosting well.

9. To any remaining chocolate frosting and white Butter Cream, add enough green and blue food color to make dark green.

10. Use this dark green frosting to frost all sides of window box. Then, with reserved pale green frosting and tube no. 47 in decorating bag, make a design similar to ours on the front of the box as shown.

Day before, make flowers, as follows:

1. To reserved Ornamental Frosting, add red and blue food colors to tint a lavender-hyacinth color, as shown.

2. On each of five 4½" wooden skewers, string 3 large whole marshmallows. Top each with a marshmallow half, securing it with a toothpick. With Ornamental Frosting, thinly coat each marshmallow.

3. Then, with frosting and tube no. 193 in decorating bag, make hyacinth blossoms, as follows: With skewer held in left hand, and starting at bottom edge of marshmallows, press out a blossom, pulling gently to form point. Repeat, placing blossoms very close together until marshmallows are completely covered, as shown. Insert completed hyacinth in window box as shown.

4. Make 4 more hyacinths, following closely step 3 above.

5. Let hyacinths dry at least 2 hr. Now, around base of each, gently press leaves into cake.

6. Set in place on table until party time. P.S. You may not only use your own color scheme for our Window Garden. Also feature it at a shower, a garden-club meeting, or for almost anyone's birthday.

118

Bridal Shower Cake

(pictured on cover)

Day before:

1. Prepare **1 package white cake mix for two-layer cake** as label directs but bake in a well-greased-and-floured 15½″ by 10½″ jelly-roll pan, about 20 to 25 minutes until toothpick inserted in center comes out clean. Invert cake from pan onto large wire rack to cool completely. Repeat with **second package cake mix.**

2. Meanwhile, in medium saucepan over medium heat, combine **2 3-ounce packages egg custard mix** and **3 cups milk;** cook, stirring constantly, until boiling. Remove from heat; stir in **2 cups blanched sliced almonds (2 3½-ounce cans), ground** and ½ **teaspoon almond extract.** Cover custard surface with waxed paper and refrigerate until set.

3. Place one cake on large platter and spread top of cake with chilled custard, leaving ½-inch edge all around. Stack with second cake. Prepare **Butter Cream** (p. 175) as directed but increase confectioners' sugar to 1½ pounds (about 6 cups) and milk to ½ cup; use to frost top and sides of cake. Refrigerate until ready to decorate.

4. To decorate cake: Prepare **Ornamental Frosting** (p. 177) as directed but use 2¾ cups confectioners' sugar, ¼ teaspoon cream of tartar, 2 egg whites and ¼ teaspoon extract; spoon about ¾ cup into small bowl; stir in about 10 drops red food color to make a pretty pink color. Spoon into **decorating bag** (or waxed-paper cone); with **tip number 30** (or small rosette tip), make borders around top and bottom edge of cake. Into remaining white Ornamental Frosting stir in about **3 drops green food color** and **1 drop yellow food color** to make a pretty green color; spoon into another **decorating bag** (or waxed-paper cone). With **tip number 4** (or medium writing tip), make decorative stems and with **tip number 67,** make leaves on top of cake. (Wrap any remaining Ornamental Frosting in plastic wrap to decorate cake or cookies another day).

5. Gently press 12 to 16 **Mint Roses** (below) around green stems and leaves on cake. Cover cake loosely with foil or plastic wrap; refrigerate until serving time. Makes 24 servings.

MINT ROSES

Up to 1 week before:

1. Into large bowl, place **3 egg whites, at room temperature, 1 16-ounce package confectioners' sugar, 2 tablespoons light corn syrup, 1 teaspoon mint extract** and ½ **teaspoon red food color.** With mixer at low speed, beat ingredients until just mixed; increase speed to high and beat until soft peaks form, occasionally scraping bowl with rubber spatula. With spoon, stir in **another package sugar** to make a stiff mixture.

2. Turn mixture onto surface sprinkled with more **confectioners' sugar** and gradually knead in enough sugar (about 1½ cups) to form a smooth, firm dough. Cut dough into 3 pieces; work with 1 piece of dough at a time, covering remaining dough with plastic wrap to keep it soft for easier rolling.

3. Between two 12-inch sheets of waxed paper, with rolling pin, roll piece of dough ⅛ inch thick. Lift top sheet of waxed paper from rolled dough. With 1-inch round cookie or canapé cutter, cut out only 5 circles. With small spatula, lift out circles; set aside. With fingers, roll some scraps into a ½″ by ⅛″ rod-shaped piece for center of rose.

4. With rod-shaped piece as center of rose, mold a dough circle around it to resemble a petal. Overlap the next 4 circles around first petal, pressing at base and moving slightly above the previous petal with each circle. Cut thick slice from rose at base so rose will stand. Place rose on sheet of waxed paper; let dry before storing. Continue making more roses from rolled dough, keeping uncut portion covered with waxed paper.

5. Knead scraps until smooth and pliable again, adding drops of water if necessary. Re-roll to make more roses, wiping spatula, cutter and fingers occasionally with damp cloth to remove sugar crystals which may form. Repeat with 2 more reserved dough pieces. Place dried roses in single layer on large tray or jelly-roll pan; cover with foil or plastic wrap. Roses store well in tightly covered container up to 1 week. Makes about 4 dozen.

Old-Fashioned Shower Cake

If you know the bride's favorite colors, so much the better. Frost **a favorite filled layer cake** that shade. Then make **tiny bouquets of gumdrops** on wires. Pretty them with a **frilly paper doily;** tie with **ribbons.** Place around cake—one for each guest if number is small—or just 5 or 6 if it's a big shower. Write a message on top with **plain tube for writing no. 4,** and **white frosting in decorating bag.**

It's Showering

Frost a **filled layer cake** pale pink, yellow, or green. On top of cake, trace the outline of an open umbrella. With **white frosting** in **decorating bag** and **plain tube for writing no. 4,** trace over outline. Then, holding same tube upright, make dashes for the raindrops. Lastly, with **leaf tube no. 68,** make a bow of contrasting color on the umbrella handle (i.e., pink on green, green on yellow, etc.). Then repeat bows of frosting around sides of cake.

Peggy's Umbrella

Day before, if desired, **make, bake, and cool 1 large pkg. yellow-cake mix** in two 9″ layer cake pans, as directed. Stack layers, then cut crosswise, 1″ below center, into two semi-circles. Now scallop cut edge of larger semicircle to resemble an umbrella. From smaller semicircle, cut umbrella handle 5½″ by 1″, having tapering curve at end. On **12″ cardboard circle,** place umbrella; center handle; trace around umbrella; lift off cake; cut out cardboard pattern, then cover with **foil.**

Make **Snow Peak, p. 178;** tint ¼ cup pale blue; reserve ¼ cup white frosting; fill and frost umbrella with rest of white frosting, making tip at top center. With blue frosting, on tip of teaspoon, make umbrella spokes: four from scalloped edge to tip; one from center of handle to tip. With white frosting go over these spokes again. Scatter **a few silver dragées** over top, for raindrops.

Cut **12″ white cardboard circle.** With **4 yd. narrow plain or variegated ribbon,** laid on top of **4 yd. wider silver or white ribbon,** form 18 loops, each 1½″ high, all around cardboard circle, stapling each to its edge. If desired, sew tiny fresh blossoms here and there on ribbon. Cover cardboard circle with **12″ white paper doilie.** Set cake on top and carry to table.

120

On Her Wedding Day

(pictured on p. 128)

Twice recipe Flower Cream, p. 176
Decorating bags, Tube no. 68, 119, 19
10 large pkg. white-cake mix
Foil or saran

Heavy board, cut into diamond shape, 26" long by 17" at widest part
10 batches Butter Cream, p. 175
4 yd. white ribbon

Two days ahead:

1. Make twice recipe for Flower Cream, as directed. Then tint most of it a delicate yellow. Use, to make daffodils as follows, also referring to step-by-step directions at bottom of wedding cake picture on p. 128.

2. For each daffodil, use tube no. 68 in decorating bag and yellow Flower Cream. On waxed-paper square, "glued" with frosting to jar top, press out 6 thick overlapping petals, which are directly opposite one another.

3. Then, using tube no. 119 in decorating bag and yellow Flower Cream, make the corona which is at center of daffodil as follows: Near center of daffodil, hold decorating bag so tube opening is vertical and its wide part at the bottom. Press out frosting, while turning jar, until circular cone is formed. Then, carefully remove daffodil, still on waxed paper, to refrigerator, until needed.

4. Repeat steps 2 and 3, making about 50 daffodils, and refrigerating on their waxed-paper squares until needed.

5. Make, bake, and cool each of 6 pkg. white-cake mix in a 13" x 9" x 2" pan, as label directs.

6. Now grease generously and dust with flour, a 17" x 11½" x 2" roasting pan. Make up 1 pkg. white cake mix, as label directs; pour into roasting pan. Quickly make up second pkg. and add to first batter. Bake at temperature label directs 40 min., or until cake tester inserted in center comes out clean. Cool; carefully remove from pan.

7. Repeat step 6, making a second 17" x 11½" x 2" cake.

8. Wrap all the cakes in foil or saran, then refrigerate. Reserve rest of Flower Cream, covered.

One day ahead:

1. Trim crusts from two of the 13" x 9" x 2" cakes; cut each in half diagonally, making 4 triangles. On a 26" by 17" diamond-shaped board, rearrange the triangles to form a diamond; with Butter Cream, thinly frost the entire top of it.

2. Now top diamond-shaped cake with 2 more 13" x 9" x 2" cakes, cut and rearranged to form diamond of same shape as before. Thinly frost this entire bottom tier, using enough frosting on the top to fill in cracks and make surface of cake level.

3. Next, from paper, cut out a 17" by 10½" diamond; use as pattern to cut two diamonds from the two 17" x 11½" x 2" cakes.

4. With Butter Cream, fill these 2 diamonds; then center them on the bottom tier as the second tier and thinly frost.

5. From the two remaining 13" x 9" x 2" cakes, cut two 10" by 6" diamonds; fill them with Butter Cream, then center on cake as third, or top, tier; thinly frost it all over.

Early on the day:

1. Now generously frost the entire cake and the top of the board on which it stands with Butter Cream.

2. Then, on sides of tiers, make this swag-like design: Using small ball of Butter Cream on the tip of your spatula, midway up side of bottom tier, move spatula in half-circle motion; repeat, directly above, on same tier; then repeat all around the sides of the three cake tiers as shown.

3. On each corner of the two lower cake tiers, and on the center top of cake, place small mounds of reserved white Flower Cream. Gracefully arrange the daffodils on the mounds, as pictured. Then, with tube no. 19 and white Flower Cream, around daffodils and along cake edges, press out white rosettes as pictured.

4. After wedding cake has been set in place on table, tie white ribbon around edge of board, with a big bow, as shown. Makes about 100 servings.

121

Tiers and Flowers
(pictured on p. 129)

About one month before the wedding:

1. Yes, a month ahead is none too early to get your order in for the **set of tiered square cake pans** which you are going to need.

2. Our set included 5 square cake pans, all 3″ deep, and of 6″, 8″, 10″, 12″ and 14″ size. We show the set on p. 182 and also tell you where they may be purchased.

3. At this time, too, check **Rich Golden Fruitcake, p. 173;** it's to be the first tier of your cake, and contains a number of fruit items you will want to buy ahead.

Measure door where reception is to be, to make sure cake, on tray, will go through it.

About two weeks before the wedding:

Make, bake Rich Golden Fruitcake, p. 173, in 14″ square cake pan. Cool in pan; remove, wrap in foil, store at room temperature.

Three days before the wedding:

This is the day to bake the four white cake squares, and you will have to make up **our recipe for White Wedding Cake, p. 174,** twice. The 12″ cake is baked first, then the 6″, followed by the 10″, then the 8″ cake. When cool, wrap in foil; store at room temperature.

Two days before the wedding:

Make **2 separate batches Snow White Frosting, p. 178.** Let stand out tightly covered. Make this **Marzipan Filling:** In bowl, with hands, blend **6 cups canned almond paste, 4 cups sifted confectioners' sugar.** If not pliable, add **cold water,** little by little, until it is. Let stand out, covered.

Day before wedding:

1. Order **a few lilacs, lilies of the valley, sweet peas,** and **allium, all white** of course.

2. Cover **14″ square board** with **foil;** top with fruitcake, bottom side up. From **waxed paper,** cut 12″, 10″, 8″ and 6″ squares.

3. On 12″ waxed paper square, with stockinete-covered rolling pin, roll out 3 cups Marzipan Filling to just cover paper with a smooth, evenly thick layer; then invert it and even off marzipan along waxed paper edge with knife. On 10″ square, roll out 2½ cups Marzipan Filling; on 8″ square, 2 cups Marzipan Filling; on 6″ square, 1½ cups, all as above.

4. Now stack cake tiers this way: On fruitcake tier, lay 12″ square of marzipan, waxed-

paper side up. Peel off paper; top with 12″ cake, right side up; on it lay 10″ marzipan square, paper side up. Peel off paper; top with 10″ cake, right side up. On it place 8″ marzipan square, paper side up; remove paper. Then top with 8″ cake, right side up; on it lay 6″ marzipan square, paper side up; peel off paper; top with 6″ cake, right side up.

5. Next, lightly frost entire cake with Snow White Frosting; let dry overnight.

Early on Wedding Day:

1. Use all but 1 cup Snow White Frosting to refrost cake, keeping corners square.

2. Then, with **decorating bag, tube no. 4,** and some reserved frosting, start at bottom of cake to outline corner of each tier, on up to top, ending line 1″ in on top tier.

3. Now, on one of cake corners, 1″ in on each side of this frosting line, on each tier, place **toothpick.** With same bag, tube, and frosting, and starting at same bottom corner, make diagonal frosting line, on each tier, up to one of picks; remove pick and make a continuous straight line, on top of each tier, to inside corner. Continue, in this way, up to top, ending line 1″ in on top tier. Repeat on other side of first frosting line.

4. Decorate other three cake corners as in steps 2 and 3, above. Next, with same bag, tube, and frosting, start at center of bottom tier to make a series of Vs up to top tier, ending each in tiny swirl as pictured. Tuck a few allium blossoms at base of each V.

5. Make **tiny bride's bouquet,** with short stems; secure in **small needlepoint holder;** set in center of top tier. Frost holder.

At the Reception:

1. The wedding cake has been set on the bridal table with flowers around its base. After bride and groom have cut first slice from lowest tier, remove cake to kitchen for cutting and serving on dessert plates.

2. In cutting cake, remove bouquet. With sharp knife, cut top tier in half; then cut each half into 9 slices, being careful not to cut through marzipan. Continue to cut, tier by tier, with these yields in mind: 6″ square top tier yields about 18 slices; 8″ square tier yields 32 slices; 10″ square tier yields 48 slices; 12″ tier yields 72 slices; 14″ square tier, 96 slices.

Hearts and Flowers

Day before, if desired:

1. Prepare two 8"-x-8"-x-2" cake pans as cake mix label directs. Make up **1 large pkg. white cake mix** as directed, adding **1 teasp. rose extract.** Turn into the two prepared pans. Bake, following label directions for 8" layer cakes, until done. Remove from pans and cool as label directs.

2. Make up **3 more large pkgs. of white cake mix** as in step 1, making eight square layers in all.

3. Now, bake **1 more large pkg. white cake mix** in two prepared heart-shaped layer pans, each of 5-cup capacity.

4. While heart-shaped cakes bake, insert some of the wrapped **Lucky Favors,** described below, in bottom of each square cake.

Early on the day:

1. Make **4 times recipe for Posie Cream,** p. 177. Use some to fill four 2-layer square cakes and one 2-layer heart-shaped cake.

2. Now cut a **16" square of heavy cardboard;** cover it with **silver or gold foil.** On it, arrange the four square layer cakes, side by side, to form large square.

3. Cut a **heart-shaped piece of cardboard** to fit the heart-shaped layer cake; cover with foil. Set heart-shaped layer cake on it, then center it on the large square cake with the heart pointing toward one corner of the square cake.

4. Now use rest of Posie Cream to lightly frost entire cake.

5. Next, make **3 times the recipe for Posie Cream;** then use it to frost the entire wedding or anniversary cake generously, filling in cracks and leveling top.

6. Now, around base of heart-shaped cake, and around base of large square cake, a few inches apart, arrange **tiny fresh baby roses, stephanotis, hyacinth blossoms, carnations or daisies.**

7. Also, top cake, if you wish, with **a few posies,** a wedding bell, a gold slipper, or the numerals "25" or "50", made with silver dragées or tiny candles.

8. In placing the cake on the refreshment table, center it, if the table is away from the wall, having candelabras or low candlesticks on either side. If the table is set against the wall, place the wedding cake at the center front, with tea plates at left, forks at right.

Lucky Favors: Wrap **tiny favors** (from jewelry counter where bracelet charms are sold) in **foil.** Insert in bottom of baked square cakes before frosting. **A coin** will bring its finder wealth; **a tiny wishbone,** good luck; **a thimble,** spinsterhood. A **ring** indicates that the finder will be the next one married.

Silver Anniversary

(pictured on p. 131)

Day before:

1. Make, bake, cool, wrap, and store **four 9″ white cake layers.**

2. With **silver paint,** paint two **1½″ brass curtain rings** silver.

Early on party day:

1. Make **1½ batches Snow Peak, p. 178.** Stack the four cake layers, using some Snow Peak as the filling; set in center of **foil-covered, 12″ cardboard circle.** Frost cake, smoothing off frosting on sides and top. Heap rest of frosting around base of cake, pulling it up with spatula to make peaks as shown.

2. Now fill a **paper cone** with frosting; then cut off ½″ from tip. On the side of the cake at the center front, press out frosting to make the figures "2" and "5". Then outline each of the figures with **tiny silver-coated candies or dragées** as shown.

3. Set the cake in place on the table; then tuck some **pleated silver-fabric edging** in place around the base. At one side, on top of the cake, arrange some **gardenias,** which are protected underneath with a circle of **foil;** alongside the gardenias, stand the 2 rings, tied with a bit of **white satin ribbon.**

Golden anniversary:

Make the **4-layer cake above,** with these changes: Tint **frosting yellow;** use **figures "5"** and **"0", 2 gold (brass) rings, pleated yellow-fabric edging, yellow flowers,** such as roses, daisies, chrysanthemums, etc., and **yellow satin ribbon.**

Double-Ring Coconut Cake

(pictured on p. 130)

1. In greased 3-qt. ring mold, bake **one large pkg. of your favorite cake mix** at 350° F. 35 to 40 min., or till done; cool in mold 10 min.; remove to wire rack. Now make and bake **second cake in another flavor** as above. (We used chocolate-chip and banana-cake mixes.) Meanwhile, tint **2 cans (about 2⅔ cups) flaked coconut** a delicate yellow with **liquid yellow food color.** Store in airtight container.

2. With 3-qt. ring mold as pattern, cut out **two cardboard circles;** overlap circles in doubling-ring effect pictured; mark overlaps on circle with pencil; cut marked section from circle; reserve smaller section. Place larger section at edge of uncut circle; secure with tape; cover with foil.

3. Lay reserved cardboard in position on top of one ring cake. Use as pattern to cut identical piece from cake; reserve.

4. On foil-covered circles, lay **four 2″wide waxed-paper strips** in a rectangle. On it, place the two ring cakes, fitting cut ring cake snugly against uncut ring and securing with two picks if needed.

5. Next, cut off enough from both ends of reserved cake piece so you can fit it snugly inside uncut cake ring, as pictured; secure with **toothpicks** if needed. Now the two rings appear to interlock.

6. In large bowl, prepare **2 pkg. fluffy-white-frosting mix** as label directs. Lightly frost one ring; refrost more generously. Sprinkle **2 cans (about 2⅔ cups) white flaked coconut** over top and outside.

7. Delicately tint remaining frosting with **liquid yellow food color.** Use to frost second ring; sprinkle reserved yellow-tinted flaked coconut over top and outside. Remove waxed-paper strips.

8. Arrange completed cake on tray; set in place for serving; then garnish with **spring flowers,** if desired.

Note: For smaller version, bake **1 pkg. yellow-cake mix** in two greased 1½″ qt. ring molds. Halve amounts of **coconut** and **frosting.**

Shower Special

Window Garden

Shower Bouquet

Preliminaries:

Cakes:

Several days ahead, in ungreased, 4″ deep, 10″ tube pan, bake **1 large pkg. angel-food mix;** cool. Make up **second package** and use to fill 4 ungreased individual 1½″-deep, 3½″ tube pans to about ¼″ from top. Bake at 375° F. 15 to 17 min., or until tops spring back when lightly touched. Cool on wire rack 5 min.; remove from pans; cool. Freezer-wrap, freeze all.

Dolls:

Buy **8″ doll** for bride, **four 4″ dolls** for bridesmaids. For tops of dresses, wrap **strips of net** around dolls — white for bride, **pastel** for bridesmaids. Wrap dolls, from waistline down, in **saran** or **foil.**

For hats, make circlets of **fine wire;** wrap each with **strips of net.** For bridesmaids', tie net ends in bows; for bride's, attach tiny **posies.** Make **bride's veil.**

Afternoon before party:

The bride:

1. Invert thawed 10″ cake; from front side of center hole, cut out crescent-shaped piece of cake all the way down to bottom of cake. In cut side of hole, set 8″ doll. Into hole behind doll, insert cut piece of cake.

2. Make **1 batch Snow Peak, p. 178.** Use to "glue" cake to **10″ cardboard circle.** Frost

Shower Bouquet

Behold the maidens and the bride,
Caught in their immemorial poses:
Step-glide, step-glide—
In angel cake and sugar roses

halfway up side of cake, pulling frosting up with tip of spatula to make up-and-down folds of skirt. For each scallop of overskirt in front, pile big spoonful of frosting on top edge of cake; swirl down side to meet folds, then up over top to waist.

3. For train effect, pile frosting on top, at back of cake; sweep it down to bottom. With **food color,** tint some of frosting **pale blue;** use on **tip of spatula** to outline overskirt and train. Refrigerate or freeze cake.

The bridesmaids:

Set 4″ doll in center of each inverted small cake. Make **1 batch Snow Peak, p. 178;** use to "glue" each cake to **3″ cardboard circle.** Tint frosting to match net on dolls. Use to make skirts like bride's, but with 4 scallops all around, no train. Dip pick into food color

used to tint frosting; use to outline scallops. Refrigerate or freeze cakes.

On Wedding-March Day:

Arrange **red ribbon** down center of party table. On it line up bridal procession. Arrange dolls' hats, veil; two bridesmaids carry veil, rest **bouquets. Candles, in holders,** and **flowers** and **ferns,** form background.

The secret: Use a big angel-food pan, a set of individual pans, and your favorite angel-food-cake mix

127

On Her Wedding Day

Daffodils bloom all year when you make them yourself

For each daffodil, use tube no. 68 in cake decorator and white or yellow Flower Cream (on p. 176). On waxed-paper square "glued" with frosting to jartop, press out 6 thick, overlapping petals, opposite one another.

Using tube no. 119 and yellow Flower Cream, make corona; near center of flower, hold decorator so that tube opening is vertical and wide part is at bottom. Press out frosting, turning jar, until circular cone is formed.

Refrigerate daffodils until needed. Peel off paper. Arrange flowers on frosted cake as directed on p. 121. With tube no. 19 and white Flower Cream, press out rosettes here and there around the flowers as above.

Tiers and Flowers

A beautiful tribute to a beautiful bride: five tiers of white cake and golden fruitcake spread with marzipan filling, then lovingly iced in Snow-White Frosting. Fresh flowers "grow" along its dazzling terraces— lilies of the valley, lilacs, sweet peas, and allium—all as delicately romantic as the bride herself.

DOUBLE-RING COCONUT CAKE—*its fluffy frosting fluffed over with coconut. Perfect for anniversary parties and other slightly special occasions*

Silver Anniversary Cake

Rock-a-bye

Whisper it softly, for the secrets' sake —
We know someone is coming, so we baked a cake!

Alphabet Blocks

Cut **10" x 5" x 3" loaf cake** in half crosswise; trim crust ends to form two blocks. Cut a second **10" x 5" x 3" loaf cake** the same way. (Or use three 6"-by-2½" pound cakes; cut each cake into a block.) Frost three blocks with **Posie Cream, p. 177.** (Or, if desired, alternate color of sides of blocks as white, pink, white, pink.) Frost top of all blocks a pretty shade of blue. Pipe letters on the blocks in blue and white, in contrast to color on blocks.

Rock-a-bye

Day before:

1. Make **paper headboard pattern** as below. Make, bake, cool **Wonder Gold Cake, p. 175,** (bed); trim ends straight.

2. Make, bake, cool **White Coconut Cake, p. 174;** slice enough off top so it's 1" thick. Lay headboard pattern on it, with bottom of pattern at one edge; with knife, cut around it. Make **footboard pattern** as directed; lay bottom of it on opposite cake edge; cut around it. From leftover cake, cut **4" long pillow.** With **Posie Cream, p. 177,** "glue" head- and foot-boards to bed; set bed on **foil-covered cardboard, 13" by 8";** adjust pillow.

3. With **pink Snow Peak, p. 178,** frost bed. With Posie Cream and **plain tube no. 4 in decorating bag,** decorate headboard with design A shown below, footboard with design B.

4. Tint some Posie Cream blue, some green, rest pink. With **leaf tube no. 70,** make pink ruffles on side of bed. Use **leaf tube no. 68** for blue ruffle, **small star tube no. 25** for pink rose buds, **small leaf tube no. 65** for green leaves. Refrigerate.

On the day:

Set Rock-a-bye on table on bed of **net, babies' breath,** or **white heather.**

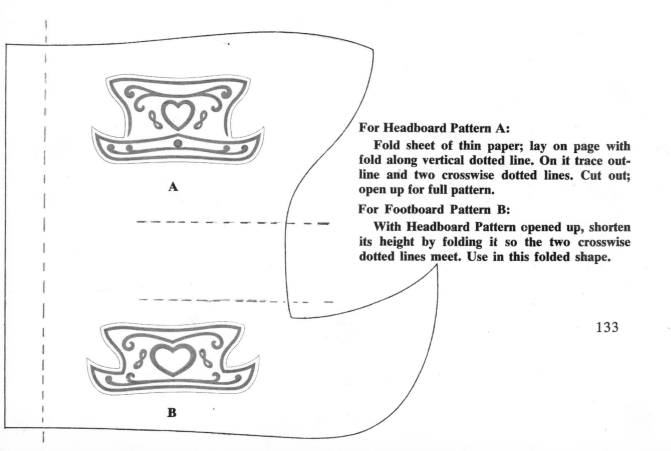

For Headboard Pattern A:

Fold sheet of thin paper; lay on page with fold along vertical dotted line. On it trace outline and two crosswise dotted lines. Cut out; open up for full pattern.

For Footboard Pattern B:

With Headboard Pattern opened up, shorten its height by folding it so the two crosswise dotted lines meet. Use in this folded shape.

133

At Guest Time
(pictured on p. 142)

The fun of cupcakes is the fabulous variety you can get from just one baking. Whether you whisk a batch together from your favorite cupcake recipe, or cake mix, you can individualize each cupcake if you wish. For example, just see how we have made, frosted, then decorated the gay parade pictured on page 141 to 143.

PLAIN 'N' FANCY CUPCAKES
(superb at any time)

2 cups sifted cake flour	1 teasp. salt
1⅓ cups granulated sugar	1 teasp. grated orange rind
2 teasp. double-acting baking powder	⅔ cup shortening*
¼ teasp. baking soda	⅓ cup orange juice
	⅓ cup water
	3 eggs, unbeaten

1. Start heating oven to 375° F. Line eighteen 2¾" cupcake-pan cups with **paper cupcake liners** (or grease only on bottom).

2. Into large bowl, sift flour with sugar, baking powder, soda, and salt. Add orange rind, shortening, orange juice, and water. With mixer at medium speed, mix 2 min.; scrape bowl and beater.

3. Add unbeaten eggs; mix 2 min. Then spoon batter into cupcake-pan cups, filling them about two thirds full. Bake 15 to 20 min., or till top of cupcake springs back when lightly touched with finger.

4. Remove cupcakes, still in liners, from pans; cool. Then frost and decorate as below, or as desired. Makes 18.

Note: You may bake these cupcakes in 36 lined 2" cupcake-pan cups at 375° F. 15 min.

BUSY-DAY CUPCAKES
(pictured on p. 142)

Make and bake **Plain 'n' Fancy Cupcakes, p. 134.** Then spread **orange marmalade** on top of each cupcake; then gently press **about 14 miniature marshmallows** into marmalade. Broil, a few inches from heat, **just** until golden.

CARAMEL CUPCAKES
(pictured on p. 142)

Make and bake **Plain 'n' Fancy Cupcakes, p. 134.** Make **creamy caramel frosting from mix** as label directs; use to frost each cupcake; decorate with **walnut halves.**

POLKA-DOT CUPCAKES
(pictured on p. 142)

Make and bake **Plain 'n' Fancy Cupcakes, p. 134.** Then make this **Vanilla Icing:** In bowl, with spoon, mix well **3 tablesp. butter or margarine,** ¼ **teasp. salt,** and **1 teasp. vanilla extract.** Alternately add **3 cups sifted confectioners' sugar** and **2½ tablesp. light cream,** mixing until smooth and creamy. Use to frost top of each cupcake. Then arrange **6 or 7 semisweet-chocolate pieces,** with pointed ends down, on each.

COCONUT-RING CUPCAKES
(pictured on p. 142)

Make and bake **Plain 'n' Fancy Cupcakes, p. 134.** Then make **fluffy white frosting from mix** as label directs; use to frost top of each cupcake. Then sprinkle **flaked coconut,** tinted with **green food color,** in a band around top edge of each cupcake.

CHOCOLATE-VELVET CUPCAKES
(pictured on p. 142)

Make and bake **Plain 'n' Fancy Cupcakes, p. 134.** Make **half recipe for Regal Chocolate Frosting, p. 136.** Use to frost top of each cupcake; then press **2 blanched almond halves,** pointed ends down, into frosting.

SUNSHINE CUPCAKES
(pictured on p. 142)

Make and bake **Plain 'n' Fancy Cupcakes, p. 134.** Make **this Lemon Icing:** In bowl, mix well **3 tablesp. butter or margarine,** ¼ **teasp. salt,** and **1 teasp. grated lemon rind.** Alternately add **3 cups sifted confectioners' sugar** and **3 tablesp. lemon juice,** mixing until smooth and creamy. Use to frost top of each cupcake. Then arrange **5 or 6 slivers of dried apricots** on each.

DIXIE CUPCAKES
(pictured on p. 142)

Make and bake **Plain 'n' Fancy Cupcakes, p. 134.** Then mix ¼ **cup soft butter or margarine;** ½ **cup brown sugar, packed; 2 tablesp. light cream; 1 tablesp. maple-blended syrup; 1 cup flaked coconut** until blended.

Use to cover top of each cupcake generously. Then broil, a few inches from heat, about 2 to 3 min., or until golden and bubbly, watching carefully so they do not burn.

GALA CUPCAKES
(pictured on p. 142)

Make and bake **Plain 'n' Fancy Cupcakes, p. 134.** Then make **fluffy white frosting from mix** as label directs; tint pink with **red food color.** Use to frost top of each cupcake.

Then, from tip of teaspoon, drizzle, in a swirl over frosting, a cooled mixture of **1 sq. unsweetened chocolate, melted,** and **1 teasp. shortening.**

MARBLE GEMS

1¼ cups sifted cake flour	½ cup buttermilk
¾ teasp. double-acting baking powder	½ teasp. vanilla extract
¼ teasp. baking soda	2 eggs, unbeaten
½ teasp. salt	½ sq. unsweetened chocolate, melted
¾ cup granulated sugar	1 tablesp. hot water
⅓ cup vegetable shortening	⅛ teasp. baking soda
	1½ teasp. sugar

1. Start heating oven to 375° F. Line twelve 3″ cupcake-pan cups with **packaged paper cupcake liners** (or grease only on bottoms).

2. Into large bowl, sift flour with baking powder, ¼ teasp. baking soda, salt, ¾ cup sugar. Add shortening, buttermilk, vanilla; with mixer at medium speed, mix 2 min.; scrape bowl, beater. Add eggs; mix 1 min.

3. In custard cup, set in a small skillet of hot water, melt chocolate. Remove; cool slightly; mix with 1 tablesp. hot water, ⅛ teasp. baking soda, 1½ teasp. sugar. Add this chocolate mixture to one fourth of batter in small bowl; mix just enough to blend.

5. Spoon chocolate and plain batter alternately into cupcake-pan cups; fill them a scant two thirds full. With knife, cut through batter in zigzag course to marbleize.

6. Bake 20 min., or until top of cupcake springs back when lightly touched with finger.

7. Remove cupcakes from pans; cool on wire racks; frost with **half recipe for Regal Chocolate Frosting, p. 136.** Decorate with **flaked coconut, tinted yellow;** or make **a yellow frosting posy** on each. Makes 12.

At Teatime

(pictured on p. 143)

LOVELIGHT TEACAKES
(always a delight)

2 egg whites, unbeaten	3 teasp. double-acting
½ cup granulated	baking powder
sugar	1 teasp. salt
2¼ cups sifted cake	⅓ cup salad oil
flour	1½ teasp. vanilla
1 cup granulated sugar	extract
	1 cup milk
	2 egg yolks

1. Start heating oven to 400° F. Line forty-two 2¼″ cupcake-pan cups with **paper cupcake liners** (or grease only on bottoms).

2. Beat egg whites until frothy. Then gradually add ½ cup sugar, beating until very stiff and glossy.

3. Into large bowl, sift flour, 1 cup sugar, baking powder, and salt. Add salad oil, vanilla, and half of milk. Scraping bowl often, beat at medium speed 1 min., or 150 vigorous strokes by hand.

4. Add rest of milk, egg yolks. Beat 1 min. Fold in meringue.

5. Spoon batter into cupcake-pan cups, filling them about two thirds full. Bake 15 min., or till top of cupcake springs back when lightly touched. (If short of pans, refrigerate left-over batter just until first batch is done.)

6. Remove cupcakes, still in paper liners, from pans; cool on wire racks. Before frosting, remove liners. Makes about 3½ doz.

PINK AND WHITES
(pictured on p. 143)

Make, bake, and cool **Lovelight Teacakes.** Frost half as **Coconut Gems, below;** rest as **Pink-Lady Teacakes, below.**

For Coconut Gems:

Make **fluffy white frosting from a package of mix.** Use to frost top and sides of about 24 cupcakes; then sprinkle generously with **flaked coconut,** or **flaked coconut** tossed with **tiny bits of maraschino cherries.**

For Pink-Lady Teacakes:

Make this Pink-Lady Frosting: In small saucepan, heat ¼ **cup milk** with ¼ **cup butter or margarine** until butter melts. Pour over 4¾ **cups sifted confectioners' sugar,** ¼ **teasp. salt,** ¾ **teasp. vanilla extract,** and ¼ **teasp. peppermint extract.** Beat until thick enough to spread. Add just enough **red food color** to tint a delicate pink. Use to frost top and sides of about 18 inverted cupcakes. Grate a little chocolate around top edge of each.

REGAL CHOCOLATE TEACAKES
(pictured on p. 143)

Make and bake **Lovelight Teacakes. p. 136.** Make this **Regal Chocolate Frosting:** In small saucepan over hot water, melt ¼ **cup vegetable shortening** with **4 sq. unsweetened chocolate.** In bowl, over **3 cups sifted confectioners' sugar,** ¼ **teasp. salt,** and ¾ **teasp. vanilla extract,** pour ½ **cup hot milk;** blend. Add chocolate; beat to spreading consistency. Use to frost top and sides of about 42 inverted cupcakes, then sprinkle sides only with **chopped walnuts.**

PIXY PARTY CAKES
(pictured on p. 143)

16 2″ Plain 'n' Fancy	1 3-oz. pkg. soft cream
Cupcakes, p. 134	cheese
Confectioners' sugar	¼ teasp. salt
1 6-oz. pkg. (1 cup)	1 teasp. vanilla extract
semisweet-chocolate	¼ cup water
pieces	

1. From the center of each cooled cupcake, with liners removed, cut a cone-shaped piece with about a 1½″ base; then make equally large hole in cupcake almost all the way to bottom. Roll cake cones in confectioners' sugar; reserve.

2. Melt semisweet-chocolate pieces over hot, **not boiling,** water; remove from water. In small bowl, with mixer at medium speed, beat cream cheese, salt, and vanilla until blended. Now, while beating, gradually add water; beat until smooth; then stir in melted chocolate.

3. Use 1 tablesp. chocolate mixture to fill each cupcake; top each with sugared cone, pointed end up. Refrigerate until ready to serve. Makes 16.

Note: Serve remaining Plain 'n' Fancy Cupcakes as desired.

136

ALMOND TEACAKES
(pictured on p. 143)

1 cup soft butter
½ cup confectioners' sugar
2 egg yolks, unbeaten
1 teasp. almond extract
2 cups sifted all-purpose flour
¼ cup granulated sugar

3 tablesp. soft butter
⅓ cup blanched almonds, ground
1 egg
¾ teasp. almond extract
Little green food color
Dessert topping or whipped cream

Day before:

1. In a large bowl, with mixer at medium speed, beat 1 cup soft butter with confectioners' sugar till light. Add yolks, 1 teasp. almond extract, flour; beat smooth.

2. Wrap dough in waxed paper; refrigerate.

3. Combine ¼ cup granulated sugar, 3 tablesp. soft butter until smooth. Add almonds, egg, ¾ teasp. almond extract; mix until well blended. Stir in food color; refrigerate.

Next morning:

1. Start heating oven to 375° F. Butter **well** twenty-eight 1¾" cupcake-pan cups.

2. Then line bottom and sides of each with 1 tablesp. chilled dough, using fingers to pat it into place; be sure dough comes only to top edge of cupcake-pan cups; smooth top of dough with fingers.

3. Then, into center of each lined cup, spoon 1 scant teaspoonful almond mixture. (Refrigerate filled ones while doing rest).

4. Bake teacakes 20 min. Cool in pans 15 min.; then invert pans on wire rack, shake gently, lift off pans. Finish cooling cakes. Serve, topped with dessert topping or whipped cream, applied with decorating tube. Makes 28.

Note: If short of pans, refrigerate leftover dough and filling between batches.

PLANTATION CUPCAKES

1 cup sifted cake flour
1¼ teasp. double-acting baking powder
½ teasp. salt
3 tablesp. vegetable shortening
3 tablesp. creamy-style peanut butter

½ teasp. vanilla extract
⅔ cup brown sugar, packed
1 egg, well beaten
⅓ cup milk
Soft peanut butter
Coarsely chopped salted peanuts

1. Start heating oven to 350° F. Line ten 2¾" cupcake-pan cups with **packaged paper cupcake liners** (or grease only on bottom).

2. Sift flour with baking powder and salt.

3. In large bowl, with mixer at medium speed, mix shortening, 3 tablesp. peanut butter, vanilla until well blended. Gradually mix in sugar, then well-beaten egg; mix well.

4. Alternately add flour mixture and milk, mixing well at low speed after each addition.

5. Spoon batter into cupcake-pan cups; fill them about half full.

6. Bake 20 min., or until top of cupcake springs back when lightly touched with finger. Remove cupcakes, still in liners, from pans; cool on wire racks.

7. Lightly spread top of each cupcake with soft peanut butter; sprinkle with some chopped salted peanuts. Makes 10.

CHOCOLATE-PUFF CUPCAKES

2 sq. unsweetened chocolate
⅓ cup boiling water
1 cup sifted cake flour
¾ cup granulated sugar
1 teasp. salt
½ teasp. baking soda
¼ cup vegetable shortening

¼ cup milk plus 1 teasp. vinegar
½ teasp. vanilla extract
1 egg
1 egg white
⅛ teasp. cream of tartar
2 tablesp. granulated sugar

1. Start heating oven to 375° F. Line twelve 2¾" cupcake-pan cups with **paper liners,** (or grease only on bottoms).

2. With knife, cut chocolate **very** fine. Over chocolate in large bowl, pour boiling water, mixing them at low speed until chocolate has melted; cool.

3. Sift flour with ¾ cup sugar, salt, and soda onto chocolate mixture. Add shortening and half of milk. With mixer at medium speed, mix 2 min.; scrape bowl, beater.

4. Add rest of milk, vanilla, and egg; mix 2 min. Spoon batter into cupcake-pan cups; fill them about half full.

5. Bake about 15 min. or until top of cupcake springs back when lightly touched with finger. Remove cupcakes, still in liners, from pans; cool on wire racks.

6. Turn up oven heat to 450° F. Meanwhile, beat egg white with cream of tartar until soft peaks are formed. Gradually add 2 tablesp. sugar, beating until very stiff.

7. Swirl a generous mound of meringue onto each cupcake. Bake on cookie sheet 4 min., or until golden. Makes 12.

At Anytime

(pictured on p. 141)

MIRACLE CUPCAKES
(plump and flavorful)

1. Start heating oven to 375° F. Grease and flour just the bottoms of twenty-four 2½″ cupcake cups, or line them with **packaged paper cupcake liners.** Sift together **2 cups sifted cake flour, 2½ teasp. double-acting baking powder,** and **¾ teasp. salt** three times.

2. With mixer at medium speed thoroughly mix **⅓ cup soft shortening** with **1 cup sugar,** then with **1 unbeaten egg** until **very light and fluffy** — about 4 min. Then, at low speed, beat in alternately, **just until smooth,** flour mixture in fourths and **¾ cup milk,** combined with **1 teasp. vanilla extract,** in thirds.

3. Turn batter into cupcake pans, filling **only half-full.** Bake 20 min. or until cake tester, inserted in center, comes out clean. Makes 24.

P.S. One tablesp. grated orange or lemon rind may replace the vanilla.

SPICY CUPCAKES
(spicy nice)

Sift **1 teasp. allspice, 2 teasp. cinnamon,** and **1 teasp. nutmeg** with flour mixture in Miracle Cupcakes; reduce vanilla to **½ teasp.**

HOT-MILK SPONGE CUPCAKES
(delicate and delicious)

1. About 1 hr. ahead, set out **3 medium eggs.** Start heating oven to 350° F. Sift **1 cup sifted cake flour** with **1 teasp. double-acting baking powder,** and **¼ teasp. salt,** 3 times. Line 2½″ cupcake cups with **paper cupcake liners.**

2. With mixer at high speed beat 3 eggs until **very thick and light** — about 5 min. Add 1 **cup granulated sugar** gradually, beating constantly. Beat in **2 teasp. lemon juice.** With rubber spatula or spoon, fold in flour mixture, a small amount at a time. Add **6 tablesp. hot milk.** Stir quickly until blended.

3. Immediately turn batter into cupcake cups, filling only half-full. Bake 15 min., or until done. Makes 24 2½″ cupcakes.

DEVIL'S-FOOD CUPCAKES
(a great favorite)

Start heating oven to 350° F. Line twelve 2½″ cupcake cups with **paper cupcake liners.**

Sift together **1 cup sifted cake flour, ½ teasp. double-acting baking powder, ½ teasp. salt, ½ teasp. baking soda, ¼ cup cocoa, ¾ cup granulated sugar** into large bowl. Drop in **¼ cup soft shortening;*** pour in **¼ cup water, ½ teasp. vanilla extract, 2 tablesp. buttermilk.** With mixer at low to medium speed, beat 2 min., scraping bowl and beaters as necessary. Add **¼ cup buttermilk, 1 egg,** and **1 egg yolk,** beating 1 min. longer. Fill cups half full; bake 25 min., or until done. Makes 12 cupcakes.

To mix cupcakes by hand, beat briskly with spoon for same time periods as above, allowing 150 full, round-the-bowl strokes per minute.

OLD-FASHIONED WHITE CUPCAKES
(lovely and light)

Start heating oven to 375° F. Line 3″ cupcake cups with **paper cupcake liners.**

Sift together **2½ cups sifted cake flour, 1⅔ cups granulated sugar, 1 teasp. salt** into large bowl. Drop in **¾ cup soft shortening;** pour in **¾ cup milk.** With mixer at low to medium speed, mix until all flour is dampened; then beat 2 min., scraping bowl and beaters as necessary. Stir in **4½ teasp. double-acting baking powder;** then add **5 egg whites, unbeaten; ½ cup less 2 tablesp. milk; 1 teasp. vanilla extract;** beat 2 min. longer. Fill cups **only half** full. Bake 20 min., or till done. Makes 24 cupcakes.

CLOWN CUPCAKES
(pictured on p. 141)

Make, bake, cool **Miracle, Spicy, Hot-Milk Sponge, Devil's Food,** or **White Cupcakes, above.**

Frost top of each with **Orange Dreamy Frosting, p. 176,** or **Butter Cream, p. 175.** Make eyes, nose, and mouth from **snipped candied cherries.** Turn each cupcake on its side, and add a colorful hat—**an inverted red paper nut cup.**

---

*The kind that comes in 1- or 3-lb. cans.

JELLY-CREAM CUPCAKES
(pictured on p. 141)

Make, bake, cool **Miracle, Spicy, Hot-Milk Sponge, Devil's Food,** or **White Cupcakes, p. 138.**

Spread each cupcake with **whipped cream;** dot center top with **blob of red jelly.** Or spread top of each cupcake with jelly; then spread sides with **dessert topping, or Seven-Minute Frosting, p. 178.** Or spread each cupcake with **jelly;** then coat sides with **flaked coconut;** let stand few minutes before serving.

BUTTERFLY CUPCAKES
(pictured on p. 141)

Make, bake, cool **Miracle, Spicy, Hot-Milk Sponge, Devil's Food,** or **White Cupcakes, p. 138.**

With paring knife, remove cone-shaped piece from top center of each cupcake. Fill hollow with **whipped cream or Snow-Peak, p. 178.** Cut cake cone in half; press into filling to look like butterfly wings.

HONEYCOMB CUPCAKES
(pictured on p. 141)

Make, bake, cool **Miracle, Spicy, Hot-Milk Sponge, Devil's Food,** or **White Cupcakes, p. 138.**

Dip top of each cupcake in **honey;** sprinkle with **finely chopped nuts,** then **grated orange rind;** or **chopped nuts** and **grated lemon rind** combined.

POSY CUPCAKES
(pictured on p. 141)

Make, bake, cool **Miracle, Spicy, Hot-Milk Sponge, Devil's Food,** or **White Cupcakes, p. 138.**

Frost with **Snow Peak, p. 178.** Press **tiny rosebud** into center of each frosted cupcake.

SHAMROCK CUPCAKES

Make, bake, cool **Miracle, Spicy, Hot-Milk Sponge, Devil's Food,** or **White Cupcakes, p. 138.** Frost with **Snow Peak, p. 178.**

Snip **green gumdrops** to form petals and stem of shamrock. Arrange in shamrock shape on top of each frosted cupcake.

LACY COCOA CUPCAKES
(pictured on p. 141)

Make, bake, cool **Miracle, Spicy, Hot-Milk Sponge, Devil's Food,** or **White Cupcakes, p. 138.**

Cut small cardboard pattern of star, tree, etc. Place on top of cupcake; sift **cocoa** over top; carefully lift off pattern. Repeat with rest of cupcakes.

NUGGET CUPCAKES
(pictured on p. 141)

Make, bake, cool **Miracle, Spicy, Devil's Food,** or **White Cupcakes, p. 138.**

Just before cupcakes are done, gently press nut-meat halves into tops; or sprinkle chopped nuts on top. Continue baking until done.

SHADOW CUPCAKES

Make, bake, cool **Miracle, Spicy, Hot-Milk Sponge, Devil's Food,** or **White Cupcakes, p. 138.**

Drizzle **melted unsweetened chocolate** over each frosted or unfrosted cupcake. Sprinkle with **finely chopped nuts** if desired.

PRALINE-BROILED CUPCAKES
(pictured on p. 141)

Top just-baked cupcakes with **Praline Broiled Topping, p. 177.** Broil as directed.

SNOWBALL CUPCAKES
(pictured on p. 141)

Make, bake, cool **Miracle, Spicy, Hot-Milk Sponge, Devil's Food,** or **White Cupcakes, p. 138.**

Spread top and sides of each cupcake with **whipped cream** or **tinted Snow Peak, p. 178.** Sprinkle generously with **white or tinted flaked coconut.**

HALF 'n' HALF CUPCAKES
(pictured on p. 141)

Cut **White, and Devil's Food or Gingerbread Cupcakes** in halves vertically. Spread cut surfaces with **Butter Cream, p. 175,** or **Mocha Butter Cream, p. 175.** Press two contrasting halves together. Or frost top and cut side of chocolate half with Butter Cream; frost top of white half with Butter Cream tinted green; press together. Repeat.

Celebration Cupcakes

Teddy-Bear: Frost **favorite cupcakes** pale green. Then set a **large gumdrop** on center top of each. On top of it, glue **another gumdrop,** placed on its side, as face. With a **little frosting in a paper cone,** press out eyes, nose, mouth. Glue on **small gumdrops** as ears, arms, feet.

Rose: Frost **white cupcakes white.** Make **one of Susan's roses, p. 28,** right on each cupcake, tucking leaves here and there.

Clown: Frost **favorite cupcakes white.** On each, make features, using **row of salted peanuts** for mouth, **candle** for nose, **tiny gumdrops** for eyes, and an **inverted little paper cup** for hat.

Rainbow: Dip tip end of **almonds** into **melted semisweet chocolate;** let dry. Or use **Jordan almonds.** Tuck **candle** into top center of **each pastel-frosted cupcake;** group 3 or 4 almonds around.

In the Pink: Top **each white-frosted cupcake** with a **red maraschino or candied cherry;** then insert **white candle.**

Sunburst: Into center of **unfrosted cupcake,** insert **yellow carnation** with short stem. Insert **candle.**

Ringling: Top each **pastel-frosted cupcake** with **2 hard round candies** with holes in center, placing one on top of other. Insert **yellow candle** in center of candies.

Floweret: Split **2 or 3 small red gumdrops.** With fingers, shape into petals. Insert **candle** into center of each **white-frosted cupcake.** Surround with gumdrop petals.

Note: For cupcake recipes, see p. 134 to 139, or use your favorite cake mix, following package directions.

Cupcakes at Anytime

Cupcakes at Guest Time

Cupcakes at Teatime

Holiday Cupcakes

Two days ahead, make, frost, refrigerate **cupcakes, p. 134 to p. 139.** Next day, make **Posie Cream, p. 177;** use to top cupcakes with "posies" below; refrigerate till party.

Nosegay: Tint some frosting **pink,** some **pale green,** some **pale blue;** with **decorating bag** and **rosette tube no. 19** center large pink rosette. With **leaf tube no. 65,** add pale green leaves. With **rosette tube no. 14** add blue posies. Mix pink and blue frostings; deepen with red or blue; with **rosette tube no. 14** add purple posies.

Grapes: With food color, tint some frosting purple as on p. 10. With **decorating bag** and **writing tube no. 4,** make grape bunch, starting at top. Lighten purple frosting with bit of white; add few more grapes. Tint some frosting leaf green; use with **leaf tube no. 65** to add leaves; use with **writing tube no. 2** for vine curls.

Holly Wreaths: Tint some frosting deep green; use with **decorating bag** and **leaf tube no. 65** to make overlapping leaves around outer edge. Tint some frosting bright red. Use with **writing tube no. 4** to make berries.

Bittersweet: Tint some frosting deep orange, some light orange. Use as frostings in making Misletoe, below; omit leaves.

Little Mums: Tint some frosting pale yellow, some orange, some green. Use green in **decorating bag** with **writing tube no. 4,** to make stems. Next, with **rosette tube no. 19,** make large yellow and orange flowers. Then, with **rosette tube no. 14,** place flowers along stem. With **leaf tube no. 65,** add green leaves.

Mistletoe: Tint some frosting yellow-green. Use in **decorating bag** with **writing tube no. 4** to outline spray of mistletoe. With **leaf tube no. 65,** add few green leaves. Use **writing tube no. 4** and some white frosting to make berries. Mix brown food color, p. 10, to paint tips on berries.

144

You Can Make Petits Fours

Four-In-Ones: All from one cake! Grease jelly-roll pan or 17½″ x 11½″ x 2¼″ roasting pan. Prepare 1 pkg. white cake mix and 1 pkg. devil's-food mix as labels direct, pouring batters into opposite ends of pan; bake about 10 min. longer than packages direct. Frost in pan, using Seven-Minute Frosting, (p. 178). Drizzle melted unsweetened chocolate over one fourth of cake; sprinkle chopped nuts over one fourth, snipped candied cherries over one fourth, cocoa over one fourth. Cut as shown.

◄

Jelly Rollikins: They're so dainty, so good. Cut a baker's or homemade spongecake layer into ⅛″ slices. Spread each slice with raspberry or cranberry jelly; then roll up into tiny jelly roll; dust with confectioners' sugar sifted through small strainer. Or spread slices with melted semisweet-chocolate pieces or marshmallow cream; then dust with cocoa or confectioners' sugar.

▼

Filled Gems: No one will guess that these dainty petits fours are made from yesterday's frosted layer cake. Cut cake into ¾″ slices. Using small cutters, cut 3 or 4 hearts, circles, diamonds, bells, etc., from cake part of each slice (see above), placing cutters so that filling makes stripe in center of each. A light cake with dark filling, or dark cake with light filling makes the prettiest petits fours.

▲

Ribbonets: Cut baker's pound-cake or gold cake into ¼″ slices. Spread 5 slices with melted semisweet chocolate pieces. Stack 6 slices to make tiny 6-layer cake. Cut into 1″ slices; then cut each slice into 1″ cubes. Top each with blob of Seven-Minute Frosting, (p. 178). Deck with chopped nuts, semisweet-chocolate pieces, candied cherries, tinted flaked coconut (p. 10), or bright jelly.

►

145

Fascinating Cupcake Pans

Square Cupcake Tins: These novel-shaped cupcake tins are not only most decorative, but, being square, the cakes pack better for gift giving. They're made of aluminum, and measure 2¾″ at top, and 1¼″ deep. They come in sets of 12.

Individual Football or Egg Pan: Whether it's football season or Eastertime, this aluminum pan bakes the nicest cupcakes. Ice singly, lying flat; or ice two together for a plump football or egg. If football, decorate icing with seams and lacings; if egg, decorate with Easter designs. Each cupcake measures about 2″ by 3″ by 1″ deep.

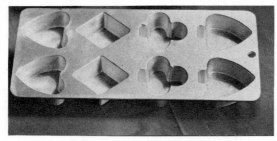

Parti-Fours Pan: Larger than the very dainty petits fours, the shapely cupcakes this pan makes are sure to be a delight to all bridge players — men and women alike. This aluminum pan measures 1¼″ by 6½″ by 14½″, and makes 8 cakes.

Individual Ball Molds Pan: It's especially for you who want to make snowballs — those luscious cupcakes, frosted and rolled in coconut. Or you can ice the balls to resemble baseballs or basketballs. Each ball is 2¼″ across, with 8 balls in the pan.

Individual Basket Pan: Tiny, and of tinplate, this widely flaring basket pan is novel for cupcakes. The tiny ½″ bottom flares out to a 3″ basket rim. There are six baskets in a set.

Individual Bell Mold Pan: Each mold in this cast aluminum pan will give you a full, well rounded, bell — about 2″ high — to be frosted as you wish. Wonderful for showers, weddings, anniversaries, Christmas, New Year's parties and P. T. A. or back-to-school teas.

Tiny Bitecake Pan: Smaller than a teacake, and oh! so dainty — each measuring only 1¼″ across the bottom and ⅝″ deep. Bit of icing on top, a wee flower, and you're all set!

For catalogues on above cupcake pans and others, see p. 179.

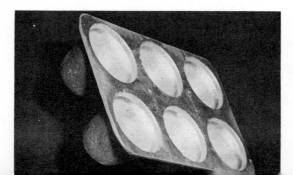

For the Bazaar

(pictured on p. 154-155)

PAINTBRUSH COOKIES

1. Sift **2½ cups sifted all-purpose flour** with **1 teasp. double-acting baking powder, 1 teasp. salt.** Cream ¾ **cup soft shortening (part butter)** with **1 cup granulated sugar; 2 eggs, unbeaten; 1 teasp. vanilla or lemon extract.** Blend in flour. Refrigerate about 2 hr. or till easy to handle.

2. On lightly floured surface, roll ¼ of dough ¼ " thick (refrigerate rest). With floured cutters* cut into shapes. Place on ungreased cookie sheets, ½ " apart. Repeat.

3. Trim as in Egg-Yolk Paint, or Pinpoint Designs, below. Then bake at 400° F. 6 to 8 min., or until set, but not brown.

Egg-Yolk Paint: With fork, blend **1 egg yolk** with ¼ **teasp. water;** to portions of it, in small custard cups, add **food color** as desired. With **small paintbrush** for each color, paint designs on unbaked cookies, as on our birdie, candle, tulip, Dutch girl and boy, etc. (If paint thickens, add a little water.)

Pinpoint Designs: With **toothpicks,** each dipped in **different bottle of food color,** prick out design on unbaked, cut out cookies.

SPARKLING COOKIES

1. Sift **4 cups sifted cake flour** with **2½ teasp. double-acting baking powder,** ½ **teasp. salt.** Mix ⅔ **cup soft shortening** with **1½ cups granulated sugar; 2 eggs, unbeaten; 1 teasp. vanilla extract** till creamy; stir in flour alternately with **4 teasp. milk.** Refrigerate about 2 hr., or until easily handled.

2. On lightly floured surface, roll out ⅓ of dough ⅛ " thick (refrigerate rest). With floured cutters* cut into shapes. Place on ungreased cookie sheets, ½ " apart. Repeat.

3. With **paintbrush,** dipped into **egg white,** slightly beaten, make wreath, Christmas ball, or other design, on cookies, as shown. Then, on design, sprinkle **colored sugar,** brushing off excess.

4. Bake at 400° F. 7 to 9 min., or till golden. Or bake plain, then outline and trim with **Cookie Frosting,** p. 163, as on holly.

MOLASSES COOKIE CUT-OUTS

1. Sift **2 cups sifted all-purpose flour with** ½ **teasp. salt,** ½ **teasp. baking soda, 1 teasp. double-acting baking powder, 1 teasp. ginger, 1 teasp. ground cloves, 1½ teasp. cinnamon,** and ½ **teasp. nutmeg.** Mix ½ **cup soft shortening** with ½ **cup sugar** and ½ **cup light molasses,** till creamy. Add **1 egg yolk,** beat well. Blend in flour.

2. On lightly floured surface, roll dough ¼ " thick. With floured cutters,* cut out Scotty, pony, etc. Or with cardboard patterns, cut out place cards in gift-box or other shapes. Place, ½ " apart, on ungreased cookie sheets. Bake at 350° F. 10 min. or until done; cool.

3. Then with **Cookie Frosting,** p. **163,** in **decorating bag,** and **plain tube no. 4,** trim cookies. Or trim with **colored sugar, nuts, sprinkles, dragées, raisins,** etc.

---

* For interesting cutters, see pgs. 164 and 169.

Petits-Fours Cookies

Here are some of the wonderful molded and cut out cookies which you can dip, fill or decorate for special parties as pictured opposite.

CHOCOLATE DIPS
(candy cookies)

2 cups sifted all-purpose flour	1 cup uncooked quick rolled oats
1/2 teasp. salt	Nut-meat halves
1 cup soft shortening,	2 6-oz. pkg. semisweet-chocolate pieces
1/2 cup sifted confectioners' sugar	1/4 cup milk
2 teasp. vanilla extract	Chopped nut meats or flaked coconut

Start heating oven to 325° F. Sift flour with salt. Mix shortening, sugar, and vanilla until creamy. Add flour mixture; mix well. Mix in oats (dough will be quite stiff). Shape into logs, balls, or cones; place nut meats in center of some. Place on ungreased cookie sheet, 2" apart. Bake 25 to 30 min., or until done. Cool. Now, with tongs if desired, dip ends or sides of cookies in melted chocolate mixture, then in little mounds of dippings, as directed in **Chocolate Dipped,** opposite. Makes about 3 doz.
Note: Cookie-press cookies may be decorated in same way.

FRENCH TUILES
(rolled cookies, like tiles on a roof)

3/4 cup (5 to 6) egg whites, unbeaten	1/4 cup lukewarm melted shortening
1 2/3 cups granulated sugar	1 cup sifted all-purpose flour
1/4 teasp. salt	3/4 cup finely chopped, blanched almonds
3/4 cup lukewarm melted butter or margarine	

Start heating oven to 350° F. Mix egg whites with sugar and salt until sugar is dissolved, mixture thick. Add butter and shortening; mix well. Add flour and almonds; mix well. Drop by scant teaspoonfuls, 5" apart, onto ungreased cookie sheet. Bake 8 to 10 min., or until done. Let stand 1/2 min.; then **quickly** and **gently** remove, one at a time, and roll around wooden spoon handle. Then fill each as directed under

A French Touch, opposite. Makes about 5 doz.
Note: Bake only a few cookies at a time. If they harden before you can roll them, soften them in oven. These keep a week or so.

SCOTCH SHORTBREAD
(wonderful any time)

2 cups sifted all-purpose flour	1/4 teasp. salt
1/4 teasp. double-acting baking powder	1 cup soft shortening
	1/2 cup confectioners' sugar

Sift together flour, baking powder and salt. Mix shortening and sugar until creamy. Add flour mixture; mix. Refrigerate dough until easy to handle. Start heating oven to 350° F. On lightly floured, cloth-covered board, roll dough to 1/4" thickness. Cut into rectangles or other shapes. Place on ungreased cookie sheet, 1" apart. Then, on the surface of each, prick out a design—bell, wreath, tree, etc.—as directed under **Pinpoint,** opposite. Then bake 20 to 25 min., or until done. Makes about 2 1/2 doz.

MELTING MOMENTS
(rich and buttery)

1 cup soft butter or margarine	1 teasp. almond extract, or 2 teasp. vanilla extract
1/4 to 1/2 cup granulated or confectioners' sugar	2 cups sifted all-purpose flour
1/2 teasp. salt	2 teasp. double-acting baking powder

Mix butter with sugar until creamy. Add salt, almond extract, flour sifted with baking powder; mix well. Refrigerate dough until easy to handle. Start heating oven to 350° F. Using fingers, shape dough into 1" balls; place on ungreased cookie sheet. Using fork dipped in flour, press balls flat. Bake 12 to 15 min., or until golden. Turn bottom sides up, and decorate as in **Black and White,** opposite. Makes 4 to 5 doz.

Bake molded, cutout, or pressed cookies. Prepare mounds of "dippings," such as chopped Brazil nuts, pistachio nuts, walnuts, or pecans; flaked coconut; chocolate sprinkles; silver dragées. In double boiler over **hot, not boiling water,** melt ½ cup semisweet chocolate pieces with 1 tablesp. white corn syrup, 1 tablesp. water, while stirring. Then remove from heat, but keep over hot water. Dip ends or sides of cookies in chocolate. Then dip coated cookies in mounds you have prepared. Let set on rack.

▼ **CHOCOLATE-DIPPED**

▲ PINPOINT

Roll or pat chilled Scotch Shortbread opposite to ¼″ thickness. Cut into rectangles. Prick out designs (bells, wreaths, etc.) with toothpicks that have been dipped in bottles of food color. Bake as directed.

Decorating petits-fours cookies

Make French Tuiles opposite, dropping by scant teaspoonfuls. As you remove each baked cookie, roll it around wooden-spoon handle. For cornucopias, roll cookies around a decorating tube. Cool; fill with chocolate or coffee frosting; dip in chopped nuts, chocolate sprinkles, etc.

▼ **A FRENCH TOUCH**

▲ BLACK AND WHITE

Bake Melting Moments opposite or other thin cookies. Turn bottom sides up. Spread with Cookie Coating (p. 163). For Chocolate Glaze, in double boiler, over **hot, not boiling water,** melt ½ cup semisweet chocolate pieces with ¼ cup white corn syrup, 1 tablesp. water, stirring. Remove from heat; cool 5 min.; drizzle, in parallel lines, onto cookies. At once draw toothpick across lines.

Gingerbread World

(pictured on p. 156)

Few weeks ahead, if desired, or at least a few days ahead:

Make gingerbread-cookie dough:

In large bowl, with wooden spoon, stir together ¾ cup heavy cream, whipped; 1¼ cups **dark-brown sugar**, packed; ½ **cup molasses; 1 tablesp. baking soda; 1½ teasp. ginger; 1½ teasp. grated lemon rind.** Then stir in **4½ cups sifted all-purpose flour** till well blended and smooth. Wrap this dough in waxed paper, saran, or foil; refrigerate till used.

Make patterns for house:

1. Following **diagrams on opposite page,** make **cardboard or paper patterns** of **front, back, gable, roof,** and **chimney parts no. 1 and no. 2,** in indicated dimensions.

2. Now, on pattern for front, draw a 2½″ by 1½″ door, with windows on both sides, as indicated. Draw windows on back and gable patterns.

3. Then, **with scissors,** cut out each one of the patterns, as well as the door, and all of the windows.

Three days ahead:

Cut and bake parts of house:

1. Remove cookie dough from refrigerator; let warm up for 20 min. Start heating oven to 300° F. On **lightly floured** surface, roll out one-third of cookie dough about ⅛″ thick.

2. Lay all the patterns, side by side, on the dough; then with **a sharp knife,** cut around each. Then, **with broad spatula,** transfer the cutouts, with their patterns still in place, to greased cookie sheets; place about ½″ apart.

3. Now carefully cut around and remove panes from windows. Cut out door, and place beside other parts of house on cookie sheets. Lift off patterns.

4. Cut out another gable, roof, and set of chimney parts from rerolled trimmings; arrange on cookie sheets.

5. Brush all cutouts lightly with **cold water;** bake at 300° F. 10 to 15 min., or until done. Cool on sheets; then move to cake racks.

Cut and bake candlesticks, animals, etc.:

1. Roll out second third of cookie dough ⅛″ thick. From it, cut out three strips, each 10½″ by 2½″. Then, with pattern for chimney part no. 1 as guide, cut each strip into seven pieces (21 in all), for candlesticks; place on greased cookie sheets.

2. With **appropriate cookie cutters,*** cut out **two dogs, two reindeer, a host, hostess, Santa Claus, two Christmas trees** from same dough; arrange on cookie sheets. Then make a knife cut from top center of one tree down to its midpoint. Repeat on other tree, but start at bottom. Spread slashes ¼″ apart. Bake at 300° F. 10 to 15 min., or until done; then cool on sheets and remove to cake racks.

Cut and bake fence parts:

1. Roll out all remaining cookie dough about ⅛″ thick. From it, cut four strips, each 16″ by 1¾″.

2. Lay three of these strips on greased cookie sheet; then, with knife, carefully cut each into fence like that in **fence no. 1** shown in diagram opposite.

3. Following diagrams opposite, cut the fourth strip into one 10″ strip as in **fence no. 2,** one 4″ strip as in **fence no. 3,** and one 2″ strip which is to be used as the **front gate.**

4. Bake and cool fence parts as above. (Leftover trimmings may be wrapped and refrigerated for use later.)

Day before:

Glue house together:

1. For "glue," melt ½ **cup granulated sugar,** stirring it until **a golden syrup.**

2. While holding a gable in left hand, carefully dip one short end of the back into golden syrup; then, quickly but gently, press it against side of gable. Repeat with front. Place on waxed paper.

3. Now, with your spatula, spread a thick line of golden syrup on the other short end of the back and front; then, quickly but firmly, press second gable into position.

4. Spread thick line of golden syrup along top edge of front. Quickly top it with one roof, pressing firmly against gables. Repeat on back of house, being sure roofs just meet at top center.

5. Now dip one long side of door into syrup; set in doorframe, as pictured, p. 156.

6. Then, with golden syrup, glue four parts of chimney together, being sure to have notched sides exactly opposite each other.

7. Make five candlesticks, gluing together four pieces for each, in such a way that opening at top accommodates candle ½″ across.

8. If syrup gets stiff, re-melt over low heat.

Decorate house and yard:

1. Make **this icing:** Into **2 egg whites in** bowl, gradually stir **4 cups sifted confectioners' sugar** until the mixture is smooth and creamy.

2. Now, with **tube no. 4 in decorating bag,** and with some of this icing, decorate house and yard, as pictured on page 156. Be sure to note that zigzag lines outline the chimney, candlesticks, roof, corners of house, gable windows, window sashes, etc. However, thin, straight lines outline and/or decorate door, roof, Christmas tree, dogs, reindeer, figures, etc.

3. Set chimney in place, as pictured on page 156. Then, with the same **tube no. 4 in decorating bag,** and icing, decorate the fence pieces and the gate with lines that simulate drifting snow.

Assemble Gingerbread World:

1. With **sheets of absorbent cotton that come by the roll,** cover the surface of a **sheet of cardboard or plywood, or a tray,** measuring 24″ by 18″.

2. On it, set gingerbread house, well back off the road.

3. Sprinkle **table salt** all over the yard to look like snow, with drifts here and there. Then carry this setup to a table or buffet for display.

4. Next, put up the fence around the house, using the three 16″ lengths for the back and sides and propping them with **table-salt drifts.** Put up the 10″ and 4″ fences across the front of the house, with 2″ piece as open gate.

5. Plant **Christmas shrubs (cuttings from your own trees, perhaps)** here and there as pictured. Spray them with **artificial snow,** and deck with **tiny, snow-covered Christmas balls.**

6. Now, place the candlesticks—**a lighted red candle** in each—here and there in the snow.

7. Make the two Christmas trees into one by sliding the one, slashed from the bottom up to center, down over the other, as pictured on page 156.

8. Place the Christmas tree, puppies, welcoming host and hostess, etc., where they can best say Merry Christmas to all those who come in.

---

* See cookie cutters shown at end of this chapter.

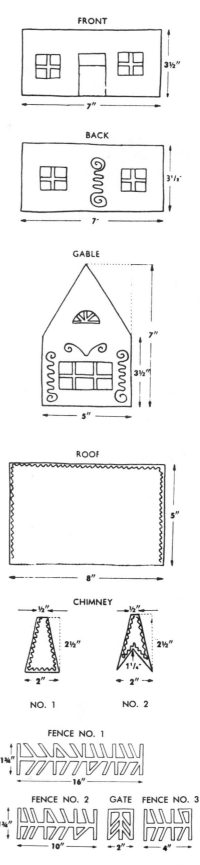

For little cooks

Lollipop Cookies

1¾ cups sifted all-purpose flour	½ teasp. cinnamon
¾ teasp. baking soda	½ teasp. powdered cloves
1 cup soft shortening	¼ cup buttermilk
	2 eggs, unbeaten
1½ cups brown sugar, firmly packed	1½ cups uncooked rolled oats
1 teasp. salt	1 cup chopped nuts
	Packaged straws

1. Wash your hands; put on apron; read recipe carefully. (Mother heats oven to 375° F.)

2. Get out Mother's mixing bowls, measuring cups, spoons, and all ingredients.

3. Sift about 2 cups flour into bowl. Now measure 1¾ cups back into sifter; add soda; sift onto piece of waxed paper.

4. Measure shortening and next 6 ingredients into big bowl. Beat vigorously with spoon (or use Mother's electric mixer) till well mixed.

5. Stir in flour, oats, nuts, Drop teaspoonfuls, 2" apart, on greased cookie sheets.

6. Make faces with raisins, candied cherries, pitted dried prunes and dates, coconut.

7. Stick 4" length of straw into each cookie, for a tie. Bake in 375° F. oven for 10 to 15 min. Makes 3½ dozen cookie-face lollipops.

152

Cookie Cottage

Cement: Mix **3 lb. sifted confectioners' sugar** with about **¾ cup water**; it should spread.

Lumber: Buy **14 3-oz. or 7 7-oz. pkg. sugar wafers,** and **1 6-oz. pkg. waffle wafers.**

Framework: On **20″ by 14″ board,** outline 10½″ by 7″ rectangle with flat layer of sugar wafers. Cement to board.

Over wafers, spread cement; top with second layer, placed to create a "brick work" effect, snipping overlapping ends to fit corners. Repeat for 6 more layers, reinforcing with **picks,** inserted vertically.

Window: With next 6 layers, leave wafer-length window space in front; reinforce. For windowpanes, stick pick upright in center of window; also one in each side, overlapping at center. Stick pick halves in window sill for faces. To complete frame, cement 2 wafers so they meet at center top of window; then add 7 more layers; reinforce.

Gables: Build sides (gables) of cottage, tapering them to a point, by making each of 14

layers ¼″ shorter at each end; reinforce as you go.

Roof: Fold **12″ by 12″ piece of cardboard** in half; lay flat on table; spread half with cement; cover with rows of wafers; dry 10 min.

Next, lift off top of each wafer. Spread other half of cardboard with cement, cover with rows of these wafer tops. Spread all wafers, on both sides, thinly with cement; sprinkle with **granulated sugar;** dry 1 hr.

Chimney: Cement single pile of waffle wafers to each other and house, reinforcing with picks as you go, tapering top third as shown. After twelfth wafer, start cutting off a little at each end of each wafer.

Finishing Touches: With pick and cement, make faces on gumdrops; set on picks in window. Outline window with cement; spot with **cinnamon candies.** Cement **chocolate bar door** to house. Add **cinnamon-candy knob,** and **path.** Set **gumdrop leaves** in **sugar drifts, filled sleigh** nearby. Set **Santa** astride chimney; roof on house. Adjust **aerial.**

Bazaar Cookies

Decorating cookies cut in today's wide variety of cookie-cutter shapes is as much fun as painting with water colors and so simple that even a child can make his own designs. The results, besides being good to eat and gay on the table, can be used as tree ornaments at Christmas, as place cards for parties, and for a host of other purposes. Instructions for the different kinds of decorations shown on these pages are included with specific recipes.

From snowy, Christmasy Sweden, we borrowed
the recipe for this holiday centerpiece.

gingerbread
world

The Cookie Ballet

(pictured on p. 166 and 167)

Baking cookies like those dancing across our photograph on page 166 & 167 is the kind of cookie fun everybody in the family can take a hand in. While some are intended for grown-ups to roll out, cut, and trim, others are easy for youngsters to make.

All are Storybook Cookies, shaped to resemble figures in the nursery rhymes and tales we all love. They're delightful as presents, as mobiles, as place cards for the guest table, and as merry tie-ons for gift packages—as well as for family nibbling, of course!

The cookies children can press into shape, bake, and trim have a special secret; they're made from those refrigerated slice-and-bake cookie rolls found at the dairy counter in your market. And all our Storybook Cookies are luscious treats, even when baked and frozen, undecorated, well ahead. Here's how.

Slice, and Trim Storybook Cookies

(Fun for young cooks)

Pocket Full of Posies

Slice: For each posy, cut three ¼″ slices from a **well-chilled roll of refrigerated slice-and-bake cookie dough.**

Shape: Cut each cookie slice in half, making six petals in all. On ungreased cookie sheet, lay petals so they radiate from a center, where tips just meet, to form pinwheel. With fingers, gently press center tips together. Bake at 375° F. 6 to 8 min.; cool 1 min.; move to wire rack.

Trim: Frost every other petal of the posy with **white Cookie Glaze (below).** Then decorate with pink and **white Icing Trim (below),** as pictured on p. 166.

Cookie Glaze: For white glaze, blend **1½ cups sifted confectioners' sugar** with **2½ tablesp. boiling water** till smooth. For light-blue, pink, yellow, or green glaze, add **liquid food color** as label directs. Makes ½ cup.

Icing Trim: For white trim, in small bowl, with mixer at high speed, beat **1 egg white** with **1½ cups sifted confectioners' sugar** and **¼ teasp. cream of tartar** about 2 min., or till mixture is so stiff that a knife drawn through it leaves clean-cut path. For dark-blue, pink, yellow, purple, or orange Icing Trim, or for blue-green or yellow-green Icing Trim, add **liquid food color** as label directs. In applying Icing Trim, use **a decorating bag** with **tube no. 4,** unless otherwise directed. Makes 1 cup.

Peter Rabbit

Slice: For each rabbit, cut three ¼″ slices from **a well-chilled roll of refrigerated slice-and-bake cookie dough.** Then cut two of these slices in half.

Shape: Lay one slice on ungreased cookie sheet. Above it, at top left, attach two halves end-to-end and slightly overlapping, with cut edges toward center. Repeat at top right, leaving a ⅛″ space between them at bottom, and a ¾″ space at top. Bake at 375° F. 6 to 8 min.; then cool 1 min., and move to wire rack.

Trim: Make Peter Rabbit's features with **pink and white Icing Trim (above).**

Wise Old Owl

Slice: For each owl, cut two ¼″ slices from **a well-chilled roll of refrigerated slice-and-bake cookie dough.**

Shape: On ungreased cookie sheet, place the two cookie slices side by side and slightly overlapping. Now pinch the outer top edge of each cookie slice to resemble owl's head and ears. Bake at 375° F. 6 to 8 min.; then cool 1 min., and move to wire rack.

Trim: Outline owl, as pictured on p. 166 with **white Icing Trim (above).** Then drop a tiny blob of icing in center of each cookie slice, and top with a **piece of citron** for owl's eye. Where cookies join, secure **a whole nut** with a bit of the same icing for owl's beak. (Or, before baking owl, place a raisin or piece of semisweet chocolate in center of each cookie slice for his eye and a piece of dried fruit for his beak.)

157

Sugarplum Trees

Slice: For each tree, cut seven ¼″ slices from **a well-chilled roll of refrigerated slice-and-bake cookie dough.** Cut one slice in half.

Shape: On ungreased cookie sheet, lay three slightly overlapping cookie slices in a horizontal line for base of tree. Above them, overlap a row of two cookie slices, letting it slightly overlap row below. For top row, lay one cookie in center, slightly overlapping cookies below. Now shape one of half slices into a rectangle, and attach to center bottom of tree for its trunk.

Press all edges of tree in place. Bake at 375° F. 6 to 8 min.; then cool 1 min.; and move to wire rack.

Trim: Frost each tree with **blue or pink Cookie Glaze, p. 157.** Then decorate blue tree with **blue Icing Trim, p. 157,** pink tree with **pink Icing Trim, p. 157,** and **tiny variegated candies,** as pictured on p. 166 and 167.

Three Little Kittens

Slice: For each kitten, cut three ¼″ slices from **a well-chilled roll of refrigerated slice-and-bake cookie dough.** Cut one of these cookie-dough slices in half; then cut one of the halves in half again; set aside.

Shape: On ungreased cookie sheet, lay two slightly overlapping cookie slices in a vertical line. Pinch one of half circles into a long crescent, and press to lower slice at the right for kitten's tail. Then press the quarter pieces, one to top left and other to top right of kitten, for his ears. Bake at 375° F. 6 to 8 min.; cool 1 min.; move to wire rack.

Trim: With **white Icing Trim, p. 157,** outline kitten's ears and tail; make eyes, nose, mouth, whiskers, paws.

Humpty Dumpty

Slice: For each Humpty, cut three ¼″ slices from **a well-chilled roll of refrigerated slice-and-bake cookie dough.** Cut one of these slices into four strips.

Shape: On ungreased cookie sheet, lay two slightly overlapping cookie slices in a vertical line; gently shape into oval at top and bottom. Near top on either side of bottom slice, attach two center strips for Humpty's arms. Shape other two strips into crescents, and attach at base of bottom slice for legs and feet. Bake at 375° F. 6 to 8 min.; cool 1 min.; move to wire rack.

Trim: Frost Humpty's legs and feet with **green Cookie Glaze, p. 157,** body and arms with **blue,** head with **pink.** With **blue Icing Trim, p. 157,** mark collar, two buttons, and little bow tie on body. On head, make two blue dots for eyes, a purple dot for nose; with **pink Icing Trim,** make mouth.

Roll, Cut, and Trim Storybook Cookies
(For grown-up cooks to create)

Roll: Let your favorite **refrigerated slice-and-bake cookie rolls** stand at room temperature 1 to 1½ hr., or till easy to roll. (Or make up roll-and-cut cookie dough from a pet recipe, cookie mix, or gingerbread mix.) Roll ¼″ thick on lightly floured surface.

Cut: If you don't have **storybook cutters** (pgs. 164 and 169) on hand, don't worry. Just draw **a pattern on cardboard** of each of the cookies below in its designated size. Lay each cardboard pattern on rolled-out dough, cut around it with a sharp knife, and transfer cookie to ungreased cookie sheet. Reroll trimmings, and repeat. Bake at 375° F. 6 to 8 min.; leave on sheet 1 min.; cool on wire rack.

Little Lamb	4½″ across
Three Fish	4½″ across
Snail, Snail	5″ across
Little Turtle	5″ across
Flowers A-Blooming	3″ across
Star Bright	2½″ across
Fat Pig	3½″ across
Chicken Little	3½″ across
Shining Angel	4″ high
Papa Bear	6½″ high
Mama Bear	6″ high
Baby Bear	4¾″ high

Trim:

Little Lamb

Frost lamb—all but his legs, tail, and head—with thick layer of **white Icing Trim, p. 157.** Coat unfrosted parts with **a little melted semisweet chocolate.** Generously cover white frosted surface with **flaked coconut,** as pictured on p. 166.

Three Fish

Frost the three fish with **pink Cookie Glaze, p. 157.** With **orange Icing Trim,** p. 157, make scales and fins. Use **purple Icing Trim** for eyes and mouths, as pictured on p. 167.

158

Snail, Snail

Frost snail with **green Cookie Glaze, p. 157.** Decorate him with **blue-green Icing Trim,** as pictured on p. 167.

Little Turtle

Frost turtle with **green Cookie Glaze, p. 157.** Decorate him with **blue-green Icing Trim,** as pictured on p. 167.

Flowers A-Blooming

Frost some flowers with **yellow Cookie Glaze, p. 157,** some with **pink;** decorate yellow ones with **yellow-green** and **yellow Icing Trim, p. 157;** pink ones with **pink** and **purple Icing Trim,** as pictured on p. 166 and 167. (Or omit frosting, decorating each flower with **pink** and **purple Icing Trim,** as pictured.)

Star Bright

Frost star with **pink Cookie Glaze, p. 157.** Then make lines on each point of star with **pink Icing Trim, p. 157,** as pictured on p. 166 and 167.

Fat Pig

Leave pigs unfrosted. Make zigzag line with dots on some, as pictured on p. 167. Top others with **variegated old-fashioned posies,** as pictured.

Chicken Little

Frost chickens with **yellow Cookie Glaze, p. 157.** Make scallops with **yellow Icing Trim,** eyes with **purple,** beak with **orange Icing Trim** as on p. 166.

Shining Angel

Frost angel's wings with **blue Cookie Glaze, p. 157.** Decorate body with **pink** and **white Icing Trim, p. 157,** or cover it with a crisscross pattern made with **white Icing Trim** and **tube no. 44.** Make tiny dots with **blue-green Icing Trim** and **tube no. 2;** make hair, mouth, and eyes with **yellow, purple,** and **blue-green Icing Trim,** as we have pictured on p. 166 and 167.

Three Bears

Papa Bear: Make Papa's overalls with **blue Cookie Glaze, p. 157.** Make stripes with **blue Icing Trim, p. 157,** and **tube no. 44.** Make eyes with **purple Icing Trim.** See p. 166.

Mama Bear: Make Mama's frock with **pink Cookie Glaze, p. 157.** Make rosebuds with **pink Icing Trim, p. 157;** necklace with **white Icing Trim;** eyes with **purple Icing Trim.**

Baby Bear: Make Baby's sunsuit with **white Cookie Glaze, p. 157;** stripes with **orange Icing Trim, p. 157;** buttons with **white Icing Trim;** eyes with **purple Icing Trim.**

Note: To hang cookies, make a hole near top of each with flat end of **wooden skewer** before baking. To tie cookies to the packages, glue a slightly smaller cardboard backing to back of each with **Cookie Glaze, p. 157.**

SWEDEN'S PEPPARKAKOR
(pictured on p. 168)

¾ cup heavy cream, whipped	1½ teasp. grated lemon rind
1¼ cups dark brown sugar, packed	4½ cups sifted all-purpose flour
½ cup molasses	Blanched almonds, halved
1 tablesp. baking soda	Icing, below
1½ teasp. ginger	

Make two or three weeks ahead, if desired:

1. In large bowl, with wooden spoon, stir together whipped cream, dark brown sugar, molasses, baking soda, ginger, and grated lemon rind until well blended.

2. Gradually stir in flour till well blended and smooth. Refrigerate 1 hr. Or, if for later use, wrap dough in **waxed paper, saran, or foil,** then refrigerate until needed.

Just before baking:

1. Let dough stand out 20 min. Start heating oven to 300° F. Lightly grease cookie sheets. On lightly floured surface roll out some of cookie dough ⅛" thick. Then, with **floured cookie cutters—reindeer, tree, star, heart, and animals** are all beloved — cut out shapes.

2. Place on cookie sheet, ½" apart. Top some with **halved almonds.** Also, if to be hung on a tree, make a hole near top of each with flat end of **wooden skewer.** Bake 10 to 15 min., or till done. Cool on sheet; remove to wire rack. Repeat with rest of dough.

3. Make **Icing, below;** then with **plain tube no. 4** in **decorating bag,** and some of icing, decorate cookies which do not have almonds, outlining their shape with lines and dots.

4. Let icing dry; store cookies in tight container; they keep well. Makes about 9 doz.

Icing: Into **2 egg whites,** in bowl, gradually stir **4 cups sifted confectioners' sugar** until smooth. Cover with waxed paper till needed.

---

* See cutters on p. 164.

159

Cookie Capers

Green Eyes:

Use **light cookie dough, rolled-out,** then cut into 2″ squares. On bottom of each square cut off 2 corners; attach to top at opposite corners. Decorate with **green gumdrop slices** for eyes, **snipped black gumdrops** for nose and mouth, **diagonally sliced licorice-stick candy** for whiskers. Bake.

Canastas:

For each cookie card, cut out 3¼″ by 2¼″ rectangle from **rolled out light cookie dough.** Bake; cool. Frost with **Cookie Coating, p. 163.** For ace of hearts, use **red-tinted Cookie Coating** and **plain tube for writing no. 4** in **decorating bag** to make letter, **red cinnamon candies** for hearts. For four of clubs, use **black tinted Cookie Coating** for numbers, **black gumdrop slices for clubs.** (To tint glaze black, mix red, green, blue and yellow food colors.)

Happy:

For each cookie, cut out 2½″ round from **rolled-out light cookie dough,** also 2½″ by ½″ strip from **rolled-out dark cookie dough.** With tip of knife, cut smiling mouth in round. Add small blobs of dough for eyes and nose. Make slits in one side of strip; fit to head as hair. Bake; cool. Insert **raisin "teeth."**

Be popular:

Send **a box of decorated cookies** to the third-grade class, via Junior—the kids will undoubtedly name you Mother of the Year.

Or, take a double-barreled gift when you go visiting — **a new cookie crisper** for your hostess, filled with **decorated cookies** for her youngsters.

Use a present as your cookie container: A **toy truck** for Sonny, a **lettuce basket** for Mother, a **fishing creel** for Dad.

Be inventive:

Make a mobile of cookies suspended by thread from a wire coat hanger.

Shape cookies into numerals to represent your children's ages.

"Glue" cookie figures to the cover of a box of gift cookies.

Calendar Cookies

(some are pictured on p. 165)

The kind that make all parties special and give young folks such fun.

1. Make, roll, and cut out our **Sugar Cookies or a variation, p. 163.** Then decorate before or after baking as each recipe suggests.

2. If cookies are to be kept for some time, or if being made in humid weather, use our **Cookie Frosting, p. 163,** white or tinted, to decorate them. If to be served soon after making, use **Cookie Coating, p. 163.**

Place-Card Hearts: Before baking hearts, sprinkle with **red sugar.** After baking cookies, use **white frosting** in **decorating bag** with **plain tube for writing no. 4,** to write guest's name on each cookie.

Engagement-Party Hearts: After baking hearts, use **pink frosting** in **decorating bag** with **plain tube for writing no. 4** to make rows of dots, ¼" apart, on each. Dip in **rainbow-colored nonpareils.**

Hats for St. Paddy's Day: Before baking hats, press into each a shamrock made of **3 slices of green gumdrops.**

Shower-Party Baskets: Before baking baskets, use tip of knife to trace basket design. After baking cookies, use **colored frostings** in **decorating bag** with **plain tube for writing no. 4** to outline flowers.

Easter Bunnies: After baking bunnies, use **Chocolate Glaze, p. 149,** in **decorating bag** with **plain tube for writing no. 4** to outline features.

Liberty Bells: After baking bells, use **white frosting,** in **decorating bag** with **plain tube for writing no. 4** to write "1776" and to trace cracks.

Sweet Firecrackers: Before baking firecrackers, sprinkle all but fuses with **red sugar.** After baking cookies, make fuses with **white frosting.**

Toy Soldier's Drums: After baking drums, frost tops and bottoms **white;** use **red frosting** in **decorating bag** with **plain tube for writing no. 4 to** make lacings on sides of drums.

Halloween Kitties: Before baking kitties, use **flaked coconut** to make whiskers, and **currants** to make eyes.

Jack-O'-Lanterns: Before baking jack-o'-lanterns, sprinkle with **orange sugar.** Make faces with **dried fruits.**

Snow Men: After baking snow men, spread all but hats with **white frosting;** sprinkle with **flaked coconut.** Use **chocolate frosting** in **decorating bag** with **plain tube for writing no. 4,** for hats, features, buttons.

Candles to Tie on the Gifts: Before baking candles, make **hole with skewer** in handle of each candlestick; insert **small dry bean.** After baking cookies, remove beans; frost; insert **strings** for tying on gifts.

Tree-Trim Cookies:

Vanilla: Make hole at top for **ribbon,** as in Candles, above. After baking cookies, use **red frosting** in **decorating bag with plain tube for writing no. 4** to trace diagonal stripes, ¼" apart, on each. Fill in every other space with **white frosting.** Fill rest with wavy lines of **green frosting.**

Chocolate: After baking cookies, use **white frosting in decorating bag** with **plain tube for writing no. 4** to make 2 rows of continuous loops. With **tweezers,** place **silver dragées** in some of loops.

New Year's Clocks: After baking clocks, use **white frosting** for faces. With **green frosting** in **decorating bag** with **plain tube for writing no. 4,** make hands of clocks and lines for hours.

Christmas Bells: After baking bells, spread with **white frosting.** With **green frosting** in **decorating bag** and **plain tube for writing no. 4,** outline holly leaves; use **cinnamon drops** for berries.

Starfish: Before baking starfish, sprinkle centers with **chocolate sprinkles.** After baking cookies, make lines with **toothpicks** dipped in **Chocolate Glaze,** p. 149.

Mr. Rabbit: Frost baked bunnies with white **frosting;** dip in **flaked coconut.** Use **Chocolate Glaze,** p. 149, for tails.

Horns of Plenty: Before baking cornucopias, trace design with tip of knife. Use bits of **dried fruits** and **nuts** to fill them.

Chicks: After baking chicks, frost with **yellow frosting.** With **Chocolate Glaze,** p. 149, frost shells and make eyes.

162

SUGAR COOKIES

4 cups sifted cake flour	1½ cups granulated
2½ teasp. double-acting	sugar
baking powder	2 eggs
½ teasp. salt	1 teasp. vanilla extract
⅔ cup soft shortening	4 teasp. milk

Sift together flour, baking powder, salt. Mix shortening with sugar, eggs and vanilla until creamy. Mix in flour mixture alternately with milk.

Chill dough thoroughly (you can hurry this by placing in freezer). Start heating oven to 400° F. On lightly floured, cloth-covered board, with stockinet-covered rolling pin, roll a half or third of dough at a time, ⅛″ or ¼″ thick, keeping rest chilled. With **floured cutters or cardboard patterns,** cut into one or more of the patterns shown on p. 164. keeping cuttings as close together as possible. Also see cutters, pages 164 and 169.

Place on lightly greased cookie sheet, ½″ apart. Bake 9 min. or until a delicate brown. Makes 6 doz.

Butterscotch-Pecan Sugar Cookies: Substitute **2 cups brown sugar, packed,** for granulated sugar. Add **1 cup finely chopped pecans** with flour mixture.

Coconut Sugar Cookies: Add **1 cup chopped flaked coconut** with flour.

Lemon Sugar Cookies: Substitute **4 teasp. lemon juice** and **2 tablesp. grated lemon rind** for vanilla.

Caraway Cutouts: Substitute **3 tablesp. brandy** for vanilla and milk. Add **1½ teasp. caraway seeds** to shortening. Dust with **powdered sugar,** or frost.

Chocolate Sugar Cookies: Add **4 sq. unsweetened chocolate, melted,** to shortening mixture. Add **1 cup chopped walnuts,** if desired, to flour mixture.

COOKIE COATING

Mix **¾ cup sifted confectioners' sugar** and **3 to 4 teasp. water** until smooth and of frosting consistency, adding a few drops more water if needed. **Color, if desired, with food color.**

COOKIE FROSTING

Sift together **1 lb. confectioners' sugar, sifted,** and ½ **teasp. cream of tartar;** add **3 egg whites, unbeaten,** ½ **teasp. vanilla extract.** Using slotted spoon or mixer, beat until so stiff that knife drawn through leaves clean-cut path. On damp days, more sugar may have to be beaten in to stiffen mixture. Use in **decorating bag.** May be divided, then tinted as desired.

IF YOUR COOKIES MUST TRAVEL

A box from home is always an event for those who are away at school, in the service, etc. But when you send cookies, use a good-sized box, fill it well, and make sure they arrive as cookies, not crumbs. Here's how.

1. Select **a sturdy cardboard packing box.** Line it with **waxed paper.** Place cushion of crumpled waxed paper or **cellophane straw** on bottom of box.

2. Wrap flat drop cookies in pairs (back to back, with waxed paper between them), in **saran or foil.** Wrap other cookies individually. Fasten each with **cellophane tape.** (It, too, comes in charming designs, gay colors.)

3. Snugly arrange a layer of cookies in straight rows in the box, placing heavy cookies on bottom. Then tuck **ready-to-eat sugar-coated cereal,** or **unbuttered popcorn,** into each nook and crevice; use enough to prevent cookies from jiggling. Top with **crushed waxed paper** or **folded paper toweling.**

4. Repeat entire process (snug arrangement of cookies, plugging of holes, and addition of layer of insulation) until box is filled to within ¼″ of top.

5. Add final, generous cushioning layer of waxed paper—so generous you have to gently push cover of box closed. Tape box shut (with **broad brown paper tape,** if available). Play safe: print address on box. Wrap tightly in **heavy brown paper;** tie securely with **cord.**

6. Label front and back with address and return address in full. Of course you'll print these clearly. (Cover printing with clear tape as an extra precaution.) Add **"Fragile, Handle with Care" stickers** and correct amount of **postage.**

7. For overseas mailing, use air express or parcel post if possible. **Metal or wooden containers** are best.

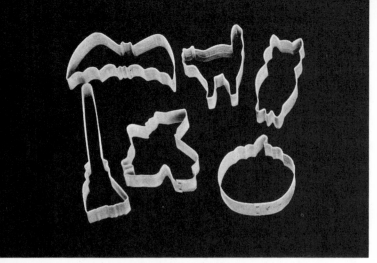

Gay Cookie Cutter Sets

Trick or Treat Cutter Set

The set shown boasts of a cat, owl, broom, witch, bat and pumpkin cutter. Another set carries a pumpkin, crescent moon, turkey, apple, cat and witch cutter.

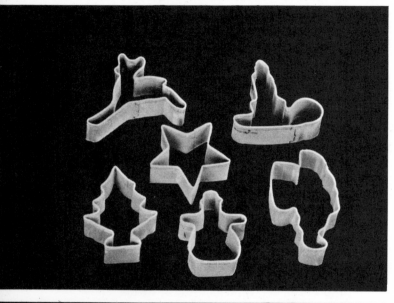

Holiday Cutter Set

The set shown features a reindeer, candlestick, star, tree, snowman and Santa cutter. Another, in miniature size, includes a tree, bell, star, crescent moon, heart and turkey.

Barnyard Cutter Set

Your children will love the horse, duck, cat, chicken, goat, swan, sheep, goose, pig, etc. which this "down on the farm" set includes.

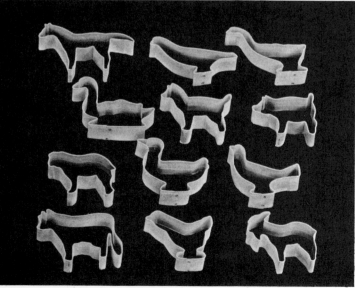

Easter Cutter Set

The three most wanted cookie cutters for Easter are running rabbit, cross, and sitting bunny. These are ideal for sandwiches too.

Circus Cutter Set

Such favorite animals as camel, seal, donkey, elephant, lion, and teddy bear are included.

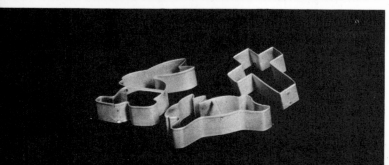

ENGAGEMENT-PARTY HEART

PLACE-CARD HEART

HAT FOR ST. PADDY'S DAY

SHOWER-PARTY BASKET

TOY SOLDIER'S DRUM

SWEET FIRECRACKER

EASTER BUNNY

LIBERTY BELL

Calendar Cookies

the COOKIE BALLET

A GALAXY OF FAVORITES, OLD AND NEW

 WEDEN'S
PEPPARKAKOR

The thin ginger
cookies (left) begin to scent
up Swedish kitchens weeks
before Christmas. Made in
gala shapes, they are often
hung thusly—on a wooden
Christmas "tree" crowned
with golden wheat. Under
the tree are Sweden's Lusse-
katt, names in honor of
Saint Lucy.

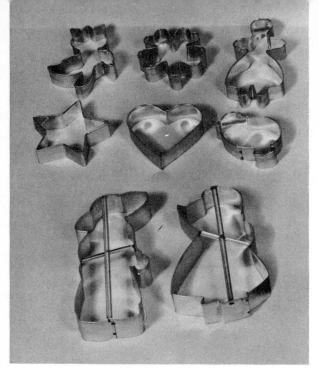

Pennsylvania Dutch Cutter Set

The set of quaint designs shown includes a prim little lady, star, tulip, 4-leaf clover, chick and heart. Below are a Pennsylvania Dutch boy and girl — each wearing a large sun hat.

Educational Cookie Cutters

There are more than 70 of these plastic cookie cutters, each with a handlegrip. They depict so many favorite themes such as old woman in a shoe, hickory dickory dock, humpty dumpty, cat and the fiddle, etc., etc. You buy these individually.

For catalogues on above cookie cutters and many others, see p. 179.

All Season Cookie Cutter Set

There are 12 cutters including a clover, fish, hatchet, heart, cross, star, rabbit, reindeer, Santa, chicken, lamb and angel cutter.

Cakes and Their Frostings   VIII

If you would share our enthusiasm for the cakes and frostings below, won't you follow these rules:

1. Be fussy about your measuring, using only standard measuring cups and spoons, and leveling off each measured ingredient.

2. *Never* alter such key ingredients as flour, sugar, liquid, and shortening, or the amounts or kind we specify.

3. Follow explicitly our making, baking, and timing directions. Of course, too, your pans must be of the right size.

APPLESAUCE CAKE

4 cups sifted all-purpose flour	2¼ cups granulated sugar
3 teasp. double-acting baking powder	3 eggs
¾ teasp. baking soda	2¼ cups sweetened thick applesauce
2¼ teasp. salt	Water*
¾ teasp. ground cloves	1½ cups light or dark raisins
¾ teasp. nutmeg	
2¼ teasp. cinnamon	¾ cup chopped walnuts
¾ cup soft shortening	

Start heating oven to 325° F. Line bottom of 13" x 9" x 2" pan with waxed paper. Sift together flour, baking powder, baking soda, salt, and spices.

In large bowl, with mixer at medium speed (or with spoon), thoroughly mix shortening with sugar, then with eggs, until *very light and fluffy*—about 4 min. altogether. Then mix in applesauce. At low speed, beat in flour mixture alternately with water, beating just until smooth. Mix in raisins and walnuts. Turn into pan. Bake 1¼ hr., or until cake tester comes out clean. Cool in pan on wire rack 15 min. Remove from pan; peel off paper; finish cooling on rack. Makes 13" x 9" x 2" cake.

*With butter or margarine, use ½ cup plus 1 tablesp. water. With vegetable or any other shortening, use ¾ cup water.

BÛCHE DE NOËL ROLL

4 eggs	¾ cup sifted granulated sugar
½ cup sifted cake flour	1 teasp. vanilla extract
½ teasp. double-acting baking powder	2 tablesp. granulated sugar
¼ teasp. salt	¼ teasp. baking soda
2 sq. unsweetened chocolate	3 tablesp. cold water
	Cocoa

1. At least 1 hr. before using, take eggs from refrigerator to warm up. Start heating oven to 375° F. Grease, then line with waxed paper,

bottom of 15" x 10" x 1" jelly-roll pan. Sift flour, baking powder, and salt onto piece of waxed paper. Melt chocolate.

2. Break eggs into large mixing bowl; sift ¾ cup sifted granulated sugar over them, then beat, with mixer at high speed, until *very thick and light*. Then, with rubber spatula or spoon, fold in flour mixture and vanilla, all at once.

3. Next, to melted chocolate, add 2 tablesp. sugar, baking soda, and cold water; stir until thick and light; quickly fold into batter.

4. Spread batter evenly in prepared pan. Bake 15 to 20 min., or just until cake springs back when gently touched with finger.

5. While cake bakes, place clean dish towel on flat surface; over it, sift thick layer of cocoa. When cake is done, with spatula loosen it from sides of pan and invert on towel. Lift off pan; carefully peel off paper. With very sharp knife, cut crisp edges from cake to make rolling easier, reserving cake pieces for later use.

6. Cool cake exactly 5 min. Then roll it up very gently from narrow end, rolling towel up in it (this keeps cake from sticking). Gently lift rolled cake onto wire rack to finish cooling —about 1 hr. (If cake is warm, frosting melts.) Frost and decorate as on p. 78.

BUDGET GOLD CAKE

2 cups sifted cake flour	mixing by hand, beat until very thick before adding to shortening)
2 teasp. double-acting baking powder	
½ teasp. salt	Milk*
½ cup soft shortening	1 teasp. vanilla extract; or ½ teasp. orange extract; or ¼ teasp. nutmeg
1 cup plus 2 tablesp. granulated sugar	
3 medium egg yolks (if	

Start heating oven to 375° F. Grease, then

line with waxed paper, bottoms of two 1¼"-deep 8" layer pans. Sift together flour, baking powder, and salt.

In large bowl with mixer at medium speed (or with spoon), thoroughly mix shortening with sugar, then with egg yolks, until *very light and fluffy*—about 4 min. altogether. Then at low speed, beat in flour mixture alternately with combined milk and extract, beating just until smooth. Turn into pans. Bake 25 min., or until cake tester comes out clean. Cool in pans on wire racks 10 min. Remove from pans; peel off papers; finish cooling on racks before frosting. Makes two 8" layers.

* With butter, margarine, or lard, use ¾ cup milk. With vegetable or any other shortening, use 1 cup minus 2 tablesp. milk.

Nut Gold Cake: Before pouring batter into pans, fold in ½ cup *very finely* chopped walnuts or pecans.

Gold Square Cake: Bake Budget Gold or Nut Gold Cake in 9" x 9" x 2" pan at 350° F. 55 to 60 min., or until done.

CONFETTI EASTER-EGG CAKE

2 cups sifted cake flour	½ cup soft shortening*
3 teasp. double-acting baking powder	¾ cup milk
1 teasp. salt	2 eggs, unbeaten
1 cup granulated sugar	1 teasp. vanilla extract
	¼ cup multi-colored nonpareils

Make cake day before using: Start heating oven to 350° F. Grease and lightly flour two 3-cup oven-glass mixing bowls (this size bowl, the smallest of a set, can be purchased individually).

Into large bowl, sift flour, baking powder, salt, sugar. Drop in shortening; pour in milk. † With mixer at low to medium speed, beat 2 min., scraping bowl and beaters as needed. Drop in eggs; pour in vanilla; beat 2 min. Sprinkle batter with nonpareils; then, with spoon, *gently* fold them in.

Quickly turn batter into prepared bowls. Bake 1 hr., or until cake tester inserted in center comes out clean. Cool in bowls on wire racks 10 to 15 min. Remove from bowls; then finish cooling on racks. Store, covered. Frost and decorate as on page 84.

* Any brand that comes in 1- or 3-lb. can.

† To mix with spoon, beat briskly for same time periods as with mixer. Allow 150 full, round-the-bowl strokes per minute.

DEEP-DARK CHOCOLATE CAKE

2 cups sifted cake flour	2 cups granulated sugar
¾ teasp. salt	2 egg yolks, unbeaten
4 sq. unsweetened chocolate	1¾ cups milk
¼ cup shortening	1 teasp. vanilla extract
	1 teasp. baking soda

Start heating oven to 350° F. Grease, then line with waxed paper, bottoms of two 1½"-deep 9" layer pans. Sift flour with salt.

Melt chocolate with shortening over hot water; turn into large bowl; cool to room temperature. Add sugar; with mixer at low speed (or with spoon), mix well. Then blend in egg yolks and 1 cup milk. Add flour mixture; mix until all flour is dampened. Then, with mixer at low speed, beat 1 min., or about 150 strokes by hand. Add vanilla and ½ cup milk; mix until smooth. Dissolve soda in remaining ¼ cup milk; with spoon, stir quickly but thoroughly into batter. Turn into pans. Bake 30 min., or until cake tester comes out clean. Cool in pans on wire racks 10 min. Remove from pans; peel off papers; finish cooling on racks before frosting. Makes two 9" layers.

Chocolate Sheet Cake: Instead of layer pans, bake in 13" x 9" x 2" pan at 350° F. 45 min., or until done.

FUDGE CAKE LAYERS

2 cups sifted cake flour	3 sq. unsweetened chocolate, melted
2 cups granulated sugar	
1 teasp. salt	1 teasp. vanilla extract
1½ teasp. baking soda	½ teasp. double-acting baking powder
½ cup soft shortening*	
¾ cup milk	½ cup milk
	3 medium eggs, unbeaten

1. Start heating oven to 350° F. Grease, then line with waxed paper, bottoms of two 1½"-deep 9" layer pans.

2. Into large bowl, sift flour, sugar, salt, and soda. Drop in shortening; pour in ¾ cup milk, chocolate, and vanilla extract.

3. With mixer at medium speed, beat 2 min., scraping bowl and beaters as needed. Stir in baking powder. Add ½ cup milk and unbeaten eggs; with mixer, beat 2 min.

4. Turn batter into pans. Bake 35 to 40 min., or until a cake tester inserted in center comes out clean. Cool in pans 5 min. Then remove carefully; finish cooling.

* Any brand that comes in 1- or 3-lb. can.

HARLEQUIN CAKE

2½ cups sifted cake flour	1 egg
2 teasp. double-acting baking powder	2 egg yolks
1 teasp. salt	1 cup milk
½ cup soft shortening	¾ cup well-chilled semisweet-chocolate pieces, ground *fine* in food grinder
1½ teasp. vanilla extract	1 cup *finely* chopped nuts
1 cup granulated sugar	

Start heating oven to 375° F. Grease, then line with waxed paper, bottoms of two 1½"-deep 9" layer pans. Sift together flour, baking powder, and salt.

In large bowl, with mixer at medium speed (or with spoon), thoroughly mix shortening with vanilla and sugar, then with egg and egg yolks, until *very light and fluffy*—about 4 min. altogether. Then, at low speed, beat in flour mixture alternately with milk, beating just until smooth. Fold in ground chocolate and nuts. Turn into pans. Bake 35 min., or until cake tester comes out clean. Cool in pans on wire racks 10 min. Remove from pans; peel off papers; finish cooling on racks before frosting. Makes two 9" layers.

Harlequin Loaf: Bake in greased, waxed-paper-lined 10" x 5" x 3" loaf pan at 350° F. 1 hr. 10 min., or until done.

HEAVENLY ORANGE CAKE

2¼ cups sifted cake flour	½ cup soft shortening*
1½ cups granulated sugar	1 teasp. grated orange rind
¼ teasp. baking soda	¼ cup orange juice
1 teasp. salt	¾ cup water or milk
3 teasp. double-acting baking powder	2 medium eggs, unbeaten

Start heating oven to 350° F. Grease, then line with waxed paper, bottoms of two 1¼"-deep 8" layer pans.

Into large bowl, sift together flour, sugar, baking soda, salt, baking powder. Drop in shortening and orange rind; pour in all but ⅓ cup combined orange juice and water. † With mixer at low to medium speed, beat 2 min., scraping bowl and beaters as necessary. Add eggs and rest of orange-juice-water mixture; beat 2 min. Turn into pans. Bake 30 min., or until cake tester comes out clean. Cool in pans on wire racks 10 min. Remove from pans; peel off papers; finish cooling on racks before frosting. Frost and decorate as on p. 55. Makes two 8" layers.

Orange Heart Cake: Instead of 8" layer pans, bake as above in two heart-shaped layer pans (5-cup capacity).

* Any brand that comes in 1- or 3-lb. can.

† To mix cake by hand, beat briskly with spoon for same time periods as above, allowing 150 full, round-the-bowl strokes per minute.

LAMB MOLD CAKE

1 cast aluminum lamb mold, 12½" x 7½"	1 teasp. vanilla extract
½ cup shortening	1¾ cups sifted all-purpose flour
¾ cup granulated sugar	1½ teasp. double-acting baking powder
2 eggs	¼ teasp. salt
	⅓ cup milk

1. Start heating oven to 350° F. Grease and flour entire lamb's mold *well.*

2. In large bowl, with mixer at medium speed, beat shortening with sugar until light and fluffy; beat in eggs, one at a time, beating well.

3. Add vanilla. Sift flour with baking powder and salt; then add alternately with milk, beating well. Use to fill part of mold showing lamb's face. Level off with spatula; cover with other part of mold; carefully set in oven in *this same position.*

4. Bake cake 1 hr., or until done. Cool in mold 5 min.; then gently loosen edges with spatula. Carefully turn onto cake rack, in natural position, and finish cooling. On foil-covered cardboard, cut slightly larger than base of cake, set lamb cake in natural position.

5. Then proceed as in Pet Quartette, p. 109.

MARSHMALLOW CHOCOLATE CAKE

2 cups sifted cake flour	¾ cup milk
2 cups granulated sugar	1 teasp. vanilla extract
1 teasp. salt	½ teasp. double-acting baking powder
1½ teasp. baking soda	
½ cup soft shortening*	½ cup milk
3 sq. unsweetened chocolate, melted	3 medium eggs, unbeaten

1. Start heating oven to 350° F. Grease bottoms of three 1½"-deep 8" layer cake pans; then line with waxed paper.

2. Into large mixing bowl, sift together flour, sugar, salt, and baking soda.

3. Now drop in shortening; pour in chocolate, ¾ cup milk, vanilla extract. With mixer at medium speed, beat 2 min., scraping bowl and beaters as necessary.

4. Next, add baking powder, ½ cup milk, eggs; beat at medium speed for 2 min.

5. Turn into pans; bake 35 to 40 min., or until cake tester inserted in center comes out clean.

6. Cool in pans on wire racks about 10 min. Remove from pans; remove paper; place layers on racks. Then turn to New Year's Marshmallow Chocolate Cake, p. 78.

* Any brand that comes in 1- or 3-lb. can.

PUMPKIN COACH CAKE

½ cup cocoa	1 teasp. salt
¾ cup boiling water	½ cup salad oil
1¾ cups sifted cake flour	7 egg yolks, unbeaten
1¾ cups granulated sugar	1 teasp. vanilla extract
3 teasp. double-acting baking powder	7 egg whites
	½ teasp. cream of tartar

1. Start heating oven to 325° F. Mix cocoa with boiling water; let cool. Into large bowl, sift flour, sugar, baking powder, salt. Make well in center; pour in oil, then yolks, cocoa mixture, vanilla. With spoon, beat till smooth.

2. In large bowl, beat egg whites with cream of tartar until very stiff. With rubber spatula, *gently fold in* yolk mixture.

3. Turn batter into ungreased 10″ tube pan. Bake at 325° F. 55 min., then at 350° F. 10 to 15 min., or until a cake tester inserted in center comes out clean. Invert; let hang in pan until cool; remove from pan. Then proceed as in Cinderella Goes to the Ball, page 51.

RICH GOLDEN FRUITCAKE

1½ 15-oz. pkg. golden raisins (4 cups)	2 teasp. ground nutmeg
4 3½-oz. jars glacé cherries, sliced (2½ cups)	2 teasp. mace
	8 eggs
1 7½-oz. pkg. chopped dates	1 14″ square cake pan, 3″ deep
3 4-oz. jars diced preserved citron (2¼ cups)	1 lb. butter or margarine (2 cups)
	2½ cups granulated sugar
1 1-lb. jar orange marmalade (1½ cups)	4½ cups sifted all-purpose flour
½ cup canned apricot nectar	1½ teasp. salt
	3 4½-oz. cans blanched almonds, coarsely ground (3 cups)
	1 tablesp. rum extract

Night before baking:

In very large pan (about 8 qt.), combine raisins, cherries, dates, citron, marmalade, nectar, nutmeg, mace. Cover, and let set out at room temperature overnight.

Early next day:

1. In large bowl, with mixer at high speed, beat eggs until light yellow and thick enough to hold soft peaks—about 30 min.

2. Meanwhile, start heating oven to 275° F. Grease, then line bottom of 14″ square cake pan with brown paper; grease paper. In large bowl, with spoon, cream butter or margarine, while gradually adding sugar, until light and fluffy.

3. Into butter mixture stir beaten eggs.

4. Sift flour with salt. (This cake needs no baking powder.) Then stir into butter mixture with spoon.

5. Now stir butter mixture into fruit mixture, with almonds and rum extract, till well blended.

6. Turn batter into prepared pan; smooth into corners. Bake 3 to 3½ hr. or until cake shrinks slightly from sides of pan.

7. Cool cake in pan, then remove, wrap in foil, and store at room temperature. Complete as in Tiers and Flowers, p. 122.

SOUTHERN WEDDING CAKE

1 lb. unblanched almonds, finely ground	2 11-oz. pkg. currants
	2 15-oz. pkg. seedless raisins
½ cup rose water	4 4-oz. jars diced preserved citron
1 lb. soft butter	
2¼ cups granulated sugar	1 tablesp. nutmeg
	1 tablesp. cinnamon
12 egg yolks	1½ teasp. ground cloves
4 cups sifted all-purpose flour	1 cup brandy
	½ cup sherry
	12 egg whites

1. Start heating oven to 275° F. Grease, then line with waxed paper two 13″ x 9″ x 2″ baking dishes; grease again. Mix almonds with rose water; set aside.

2. In large bowl, with mixer at medium speed, blend butter with sugar; then add egg yolks; beat well. Now beat in half of flour; keep beating till well blended.

3. In very large kettle, place currants, raisins, and citron; then add remaining flour, nutmeg, cinnamon, and cloves. Using hands, toss this mixture together until all fruits are well coated with the spicy flour; next, mix in almonds, brandy, sherry, then butter mixture. Last, with spoon, blend in egg whites, beaten stiff.

4. Divide cake batter between two prepared baking dishes. Place small pan of hot water (it helps keep cakes moist) in 275° F. oven. Then bake cakes 2 to 2¼ hr., or until cake tester, inserted in center of each, comes out clean.

5. Cool cakes completely in pans; then remove waxed paper. (Now, if desired, brush cakes with fruit juice, cider, sherry, or brandy —about 3 tablesp. per cake—or saturate a cloth with one of these and use to wrap cakes.) Wrap them tightly in waxed paper, saran, or foil; refrigerate. Frost and decorate as shown on p. 33.

VALENTINE LAYER CAKE

2¼ cups sifted cake flour	½ cup soft shortening*
1½ cups granulated sugar	¾ cup milk
4 teasp. double-acting baking powder	1 teasp. vanilla extract
1 teasp. salt	¾ teasp. almond extract
	4 egg whites, unbeaten
	¼ cup milk

1. Start heating oven to 350° F. Grease, then line with waxed paper, bottoms of two 1½"-deep 9" layer cake pans.

2. Into large bowl, sift flour, sugar, baking powder, and salt. Drop in shortening; pour in ¾ cup milk and extracts.

3. With mixer at medium speed, beat for 2 min., scraping bowl and beaters occasionally as needed.

4. Add egg whites and ¼ cup milk; beat for 2 min. Turn batter into prepared pans.

5. Bake for 20 min., or till cake tester, inserted in center, comes out clean.

6. On cake racks, cool cake layers in pans for 10 to 15 min. Then, with spatula, loosen edges. Place rack over top of each layer; invert pan and rack together; place on table.

7. Lift off pan; remove waxed paper. Place a second rack lightly on bottom of each layer; invert both racks with layer to turn it right side up. Finish cooling. Frost and decorate as on p. 84.

* Any brand that comes in 1- or 3-lb. can.

WHITE COCONUT CAKE

2 cups sifted cake flour	½ teasp. vanilla extract
1¼ cups granulated sugar	¼ teasp. almond extract
1½ teasp. double-acting baking powder	4 medium egg whites, unbeaten
1 teasp. salt	½ cup snipped flaked coconut or chopped nuts
½ cup soft shortening*	
½ cup milk	

Make cake day before using: Start heating oven to 350° F. Grease, then line with waxed paper, bottom of 9" x 9" x 2" pan.

Into large bowl, sift flour, sugar, baking powder, salt. Drop in shortening; pour in milk and extracts. † With mixer at medium speed, beat 2 min., scraping bowl and beaters as needed. Add egg whites; beat 2 min. Fold in coconut. Turn into pan. Bake 30 to 35 min., or until cake tester inserted in center comes out clean. Cool in pan on wire rack 10 min. Remove from pan; peel off paper; then finish cooling on rack. Store, covered.

* Any brand that comes in 1- or 3-lb. can.

† To mix with spoon, beat briskly for same time periods as with mixer. Allow 150 full, round-the-bowl strokes per minute.

WHITE WEDDING CAKE

7½ cups sifted cake flour	1⅔ cups soft shortening*
8¼ teasp. double-acting baking powder	4 cups granulated sugar
2 teasp. salt	2½ cups milk
6", 8", 10" and 12" square pans, 3" deep	12 egg whites
	⅓ cup granulated sugar

1. Sift flour with baking powder and salt. Grease, then flour, bottom of each of square pans. Start heating oven to 350°F.

2. In large bowl, with mixer at medium speed, cream shortening while *gradually* adding 4 cups granulated sugar until very light and fluffy; transfer mixture to 8-qt. pan. Now alternately mix in flour mixture and milk, starting and ending with flour mixture.

3. In large bowl, with mixer at high speed, or with wire whip, beat egg whites until they foam; then gradually beat in ⅓ cup granulated sugar, while beating until they are stiff; fold into batter.

4. Fill 6" cake pan half full of batter; refrigerate. Fill 12" pan with rest of batter; bake 1 hr. or until cake tester inserted in center comes out clean; cool on wire racks about 30 min.; then remove from pan and finish cooling. When cool, wrap in foil, and store at room temperature.

5. Now bake 6" cake 1 hr., or until cake tester inserted in center comes out clean; then cool, remove from pan, wrap, and store as in step 4 above.

6. Make up White Wedding Cake batter once again. Fill 8" pan half full of batter; refrigerate. Fill 10" pan with remaining batter; bake 1 hr., or until cake tester inserted in center comes out clean; then cool, remove from pan, and wrap and store as in step 4 above.

7. Bake 8″ cake 1 hr., or until cake tester inserted in center comes out clean; then cool, remove from pan, wrap, and store as in step 4 above. Complete as in Tiers and Flowers, p. 122.

* Any brand that comes in 1- or 3-lb. can.

WONDER GOLD CAKE

2¼ cups sifted cake flour	½ cup soft shortening*
2 teasp. double-acting baking powder	5 medium egg yolks, unbeaten
¾ teasp. salt	1 teasp. vanilla extract; or 2 teasp. grated orange rind
1 cup granulated sugar	
½ teasp. mace	¾ cup milk

Make cake day before using: Start heating oven to 350° F. Grease, then line with waxed paper, bottom of 10″ x 5″ x 3″ loaf pan.

Into large bowl, sift flour, baking powder, salt, sugar, mace. Drop in shortening, egg yolks; pour in vanilla, half of milk. † With mixer at low to medium speed, beat until all flour is dampened; then beat 2 min., scraping bowl and beaters as needed. Pour in rest of milk; beat 1 min. Turn into pan. Bake 1 hr. to 1 hr. 10 min., or until cake tester inserted in center comes out clean. (Top of cake will crack.) Cool in pan on wire rack 10 to 15 min. Remove from pan; then finish cooling on rack. Store, covered.

* Any brand that comes in 1- or 3-lb. can.

† To mix with spoon, beat briskly for same time periods as with mixer. Allow 150 full, round-the-bowl strokes per minute.

Frostings

BLOSSOM FROSTING

1 teasp. unflavored gelatine	½ cup heavy cream
¼ cup granulated sugar	1½ cups heavy cream
	About 6 drops red food color

In small saucepan, mix gelatine with sugar. Add ½ cup heavy cream; stir until blended. Then heat, stirring constantly, until mixture is completely smooth, with no undissolved gelatine. Let cool.

In medium bowl, with egg beater, beat 1½ cups heavy cream with gelatine mixture until slightly thickened. Add red food color to tint delicate pink; then continue beating until mixture is of spreading consistency. Refrigerate.

BUTTER CREAM

1 lb. confectioners' sugar, sifted	½ teasp. salt
½ cup soft shortening	⅓ cup milk
2 tablesp. butter or margarine	1½ teasp. vanilla extract
	½ teasp. almond extract

In large bowl, with mixer at low speed, mix sugar, shortening, butter, and salt until smooth. Gradually beat in combined milk and extracts, then beat until smooth and of spreading consistency.

Mocha: With sugar, sift ½ cup cocoa, 1 teasp. instant coffee.

CARNATION-PINK FROSTING

1 10½-oz. pkg. frozen sliced strawberries, thawed	¼ cup granulated sugar
¼ teasp. salt	⅓ cup white corn syrup
2 egg whites	1 teasp. vanilla extract

1. Drain thawed strawberries well, reserving juice.

2. In small bowl, place salt and egg whites. With mixer at high speed, beat until soft peaks form.

3. At low speed, gradually add sugar, and continue beating until smooth and glossy. Slowly add corn syrup, while beating constantly. Then slowly beat in ⅓ cup reserved strawberry juice, and beat till stiff. Add drained strawberries, vanilla extract; beat till of spreading consistency.

CHOCOLATE BUTTER CREAM

¼ lb. butter or margarine	3 sq. unsweetened chocolate, melted
⅛ teasp. salt	¼ cup milk or light cream
3½ cups sifted confectioners' sugar	1½ teasp. vanilla extract
2 egg yolks, unbeaten	

With mixer at medium speed (or with spoon) thoroughly mix butter or margarine with salt and 1 cup sifted confectioners' sugar until light and fluffy. Add egg yolks, and melted chocolate; then add 2½ cups sifted confectioners' sugar, milk, and vanilla, beating until very smooth and of spreading consistency. Cover until ready to use.

CHOCOLATE BUTTER FROSTING

½ cup butter or margarine	1½ teasp. vanilla extract
⅛ teasp. salt	3 sq. unsweetened chocolate, melted
3½ cups sifted confectioners' sugar	About 2 tablesp. light cream or milk
1 egg, unbeaten	

1. In small bowl, with mixer at medium speed, thoroughly mix butter, salt, 1 cup confectioners' sugar till light and fluffy.

2. Blend in egg, vanilla, and chocolate. While beating till very smooth, gradually add rest of sugar and enough cream to make frosting of spreading consistency.

CHOCOLATE CHIP WHIPPED CREAM

1 6-oz. pkg. semisweet chocolate pieces	2 tablesp. cold water
½ teasp. unflavored gelatine	1 cup heavy cream
	Speck salt
	2 tablesp. confectioners' sugar

Melt chocolate over *hot, not boiling,* water; then let cool. In small bowl, soften gelatine in cold water. Meanwhile, scald 2 tablesp. cream; add to gelatine while stirring till dissolved; refrigerate. When thick, *but not set,* beat with egg beater till frothy. Whip remaining cream; add salt, sugar; fold in gelatine mixture. Then fold in *cooled,* melted chocolate. After spreading on cake, serve soon; and refrigerate any leftovers.

CLOWN CREAM

In small bowl with mixer at low speed, blend about *1 cup sifted confectioners' sugar* with *¼ cup soft shortening, 2 teasp. milk, few drops vanilla extract,* and *dash salt* until smooth, creamy, and spreadable. Cover, let stand out until ready to use.

DAD'S FAVORITE FUDGE FROSTING

With mixer at medium speed, thoroughly mix together *⅔ cup soft butter; about 3 cups sifted confectioners' sugar; 2 eggs; 2 sq. unsweetened chocolate, melted;* and *1 teasp. vanilla extract.* Continue to beat at medium speed until the mixture is very smooth and has a spreading consistency.

DATE FILLING

Snip *1 8-oz. pkg. pitted dates.* In saucepan, combine dates, *½ cup water,* and *dash salt.*

Cook, stirring, until all the water is absorbed. Cool. Then stir in 2 tablesp. brandy.

DREAMY FROSTING

2 3-oz. pkg. soft cream cheese	About 4½ cups sifted confectioners' sugar
2 tablesp. milk or light cream	Dash salt
	1 teasp. vanilla extract

Blend cheese with milk. Slowly stir in sugar, then salt, vanilla. Blend well.

Fills and frosts two 8″ or 9″ layers. Halve recipe to frost 8″ x 8″ x 2″ or 9″ x 9″ x 2″ cake.

Chocolate: To cheese, add 2 sq. slightly cooled, melted unsweetened chocolate; increase milk to 3 tablesp., if necessary.

Orange: Substitute orange juice for milk, 1 teasp. grated orange rind for vanilla.

Coffee: With sugar, add 4 teasp. instant coffee.

Date-Nut: Add ½ cup each chopped dates and chopped walnuts.

Lemon: Substitute lemon juice for milk. Omit vanilla. Add 2 teasp. grated lemon rind.

FLOWER CREAM

About 1 lb. confectioners' sugar, sifted	¾ teasp. salt
¾ cup plus 2 tablesp. soft shortening	5 teasp. milk
2 tablesp. butter or margarine	1½ teasp. vanilla extract
	½ teasp. almond extract

In large bowl, with mixer at *low* speed, beat ingredients smooth.

Chocolate: Add 1½ cups sifted cocoa, ½ to 1 teasp. red food color; increase milk to 6 tablesp.

HUNGARIAN CHOCOLATE FROSTING

6 sq. unsweetened chocolate, melted	¼ cup hot water
3 cups sifted confectioners' sugar	2 eggs*
	½ cup soft butter or margarine

1. Combine chocolate, sugar and water. Add eggs, one at a time, beating well with mixer or spoon after each addition.

2. Add butter, one tablesp. at a time, beating until thick enough to spread.

* For a richer frosting, substitute 6 egg yolks for eggs and increase hot water to 5 tablesp.

MAY DAY FROSTING

In large bowl, blend *¾ cup very soft butter or margarine* with *1¾ cups shortening*, till smooth. Add *1 cup sifted confectioners' sugar, ⅛ teasp. salt;* mix smooth. Add *1 unbeaten egg white, 1¼ cups sifted confectioners' sugar, 1 teasp. almond extract;* mix smooth. Cover; let stand at room temperature till needed.

If holding frosting until next day before using, check it first for consistency; if too soft add a little sifted confectioners' sugar; if too stiff, add a little egg white or cold water.

NO-COOK MARSHMALLOW FROSTING

In small bowl, place *¼ teasp. salt* and *2 egg whites*. With mixer at high speed, beat until whites form soft peaks. Add *¼ cup granulated sugar*, a tablespoonful at a time, beating until smooth and glossy. Slowly add *¾ cup white corn syrup*, beating thoroughly after each addition; then beat until frosting forms firm peaks. Fold in *1¼ teasp. vanilla extract*. Tint if desired. When storing cake frosted with this frosting, do not cover.

ORANGE BUTTER CREAM

½ cup soft butter, margarine, or shortening	confectioners' sugar
⅛ teasp. salt	2 unbeaten egg yolks
About 3½ cups sifted	1 teasp. grated orange rind
	About 2 tablesp. milk

With your mixer at medium speed (or with spoon), thoroughly mix butter with salt and 1 cup confectioners' sugar until light and fluffy. Add egg yolks, rind, and part of milk; beat well. Add, alternately, rest of sugar and milk, beating till very smooth and of spreading consistency.

ORNAMENTAL FROSTING

About 2 1-lb. pkg. confectioners' sugar	6 egg whites
1 teasp. cream of tartar	1 teasp. vanilla or almond extract

Sift sugar, cream of tartar through very fine sieve. Add egg whites; mix, using mixer. Add vanilla. Beat so stiff that knife drawn through leaves clean-cut path, adding sugar if needed (on damp days, you may need to beat in more sugar to stiffen frosting). To store, cover top of frosting completely with damp, clean cloth wrung free of all water; refrigerate.

P.S. If two batches are needed, make one at a time, as directed.

PARTY CREAM

About 1½ cups sifted confectioners' sugar	3 tablesp. butter or margarine
¼ cup shortening	½ teasp. vanilla extract
	Pinch salt

In small bowl, with mixer at low speed (or with spoon), combine all ingredients; beat until fluffy; then use as directed.

PINK CAMELLIA CREAM

1 cup soft vegetable shortening	1 egg white, unbeaten
About 2½ cups sifted confectioners' sugar	¼ teasp. vanilla extract
¼ teasp. salt	¼ teasp. almond extract
2 tablesp. cornstarch	Liquid red food color

1. In bowl, with mixer at low speed, mix shortening *just* until smooth. Add half of confectioners' sugar, salt, and cornstarch; continue to mix at low speed *just* until smooth.

2. Now add egg white, extracts, and rest of confectioners' sugar or enough to make mixture so stiff that a knife drawn through it leaves a clean-cut path; mix again at low speed until smooth. Then tint cream pastel-pink with few drops liquid red food color.

PRALINE BROILED TOPPING

Combine well *⅓ cup melted butter, margarine, or shortening; ½ cup brown sugar, packed; ¼ cup milk; dash salt; ½ teasp. vanilla extract; 1 cup snipped flaked coconut.* Spread over top of each just-baked cupcake. Broil slowly until golden, watching carefully to prevent coconut from burning (about 5 min.).

POSIE CREAM

1 cup vegetable shortening	¼ cup soft butter or margarine
⅛ teasp. salt	1½ teasp. vanilla extract, or 1 teasp. almond extract
About 3 cups sifted confectioners' sugar	

With mixer at low speed, mix shortening, salt, 1 cup sugar, butter, and vanilla until smooth; then gradually beat in rest of sugar, and beat until of spreading consistency.

Especially nice to use in a decorating bag to bedeck birthday, wedding and other cakes. Keeps soft several days if stored, covered, at room temperature.

Coffee: Add 1 tablesp. instant coffee, dissolved in 1 tablesp. water.

Chocolate: Make half recipe; then beat in ⅔ cup sifted cocoa.

RANGE FROSTING

2 cups dark corn syrup	Pinch salt
3 egg whites	1½ teasp. vanilla extract

1. In small saucepan, heat corn syrup till boiling.

2. With mixer or egg beater, beat egg whites until they form soft peaks when beater is raised.

3. Add pinch of salt. Then slowly pour in corn syrup, continuing to beat until frosting is fluffy and forms peaks when beater is raised. Fold in vanilla.

RED BUTTER-CREAM FROSTING

1 cup soft shortening*	1½ teasp. vanilla or
⅛ teasp. salt	almond extract
About 3 cups sifted	3½ 1-oz. bottles paste
confectioners' sugar	red food color (5
¼ cup soft butter	tablesp. plus ¾
	teasp.)

With mixer at medium speed, thoroughly mix shortening with salt and ½ cup confectioners' sugar till light and fluffy. Add rest of sugar and butter alternately, beating till very smooth and of spreading consistency; add vanilla. Blend in food color. Store at room temperature.

* Any brand that comes in 1- or 3-lb. can.

"SEVEN-MINUTE" FROSTING

2 egg whites	1 tablesp. white corn
1½ cups granulated	syrup
sugar	½ teasp. salt
½ cup water*	1 teasp. vanilla extract

In double-boiler top, combine all ingredients except vanilla. With mixer at high speed, beat about 1 min. to blend; then place over *rapidly boiling* water, and beat till mixture forms peaks when beater is raised (don't be surprised if this takes more than 7 min.). Remove from boiling water (for smoothest frosting, empty into large bowl). Add vanilla; continue beating until thick enough to spread.

Generously fills and frosts two 8″ or 9″ layers; or frosts 10″ sponge, angel, or chiffon cake, or 13″ x 9″ x 2″ cake, or 2 doz. cupcakes.

* For crusty surface, reduce water to ⅓ cup.

SNOW CREAM

In bowl, with mixer at low speed, blend *1 cup sifted confectioners' sugar, ¼ cup soft shortening, 2 teasp. milk, few drops vanilla extract, dash salt.* Makes about ⅔ cup.

SNOW PEAK

1¼ cups white corn	2 egg whites
syrup	Pinch salt
	1 teasp. vanilla extract

In small saucepan, heat corn syrup till boiling. With mixer at high speed, or with egg beater, beat egg whites until they form soft peaks when beater is raised. Add salt. Slowly pour in syrup, continuing to beat until frosting is fluffy and forms peaks when beater is raised. Fold in vanilla.

Fills and frosts two 8″ or 9″ layers.

Chocolate Snow Peak: Fold in 2 sq. melted unsweetened chocolate with vanilla.

Maple Snow Peak: Substitute dark corn syrup for white corn syrup, also ½ teasp. each of vanilla and maple extracts for vanilla.

SNOW-WHITE FROSTING

2 lb. sifted confectioners'	2 tablesp. butter or
sugar	margarine
¾ cup plus 2 tablesp.	1 teasp. salt
soft vegetable	⅔ cup milk
shortening	1 teasp. almond extract
	1 teasp. vanilla extract

In large bowl, combine sugar, shortening, butter, salt, milk, extracts. With mixer at low speed, beat just till smooth. Cover with foil till ready to use. Makes 4½ cups.

SWEETHEART FROSTING

1⅓ cups white corn	½ teasp. vanilla extract
syrup	Liquid red food color
2 egg whites	Canned flaked coconut
Dash salt	or grated fresh
½ teasp. almond	coconut
extract	

1. In small saucepan, heat corn syrup until boiling.

2. With mixer or egg beater, beat egg whites until they form soft peaks when mixer is raised.

3. Add salt. Then slowly pour in hot corn syrup, continuing to beat until frosting is fluffy and forms peaks when mixer is raised. Fold in extracts.

4. Tint frosting pastel pink with red food color. Use to fill cake layers, then to swirl over sides and top as on p. 87.

5. Now sprinkle coconut over sides and top of frosted cake.

178

YUMMY CHOCOLATE FROSTING

1 cup sifted
   confectioners' sugar
1 egg or 2 egg yolks,
   unbeaten*
¼ cup milk

½ teasp. vanilla extract
4 sq. unsweetened
   chocolate, melted
1 tablesp. soft butter
   or margarine

Combine all the ingredients. Then, with mixer at medium speed, beat until stiff enough to spread—about 5 min. (If weather is warm, set bowl of frosting in bowl of ice or ice water and beat. Or refrigerate a short while before beating.) Fills and frosts two 9″ layers.

* Yolks make deeper-colored frosting.

Decorating Utensils and Cake Pans

A number of the special ingredients, utensils, pans and other baking and decorating materials you will need for making and decorating the cakes in this book will be found in supermarkets, variety stores or in the housewares section of department stores. Or you may write for the catalogues of the following cake decorating supply houses:

YUMMY STRAWBERRY GLAZE

2 egg yolks, beaten
2 tablesp. soft butter
   or margarine
3 cups sifted confec-
   tioners' sugar

About ½ cup
   crushed, thawed
   frozen straw-
   berries

Stir yolks into butter. Alternately add sugar and berries (glaze should run down sides of cake). Nice for 10″ angel or sponge cake.

Pineapple: Substitute ½ cup drained canned crushed pineapple for strawberries.

Orange: Substitute ¼ cup orange juice and 3 tablesp. grated orange rind for strawberries.

Maid of Scandinavia Company, 3245 Raleigh Avenue, Minneapolis, Minn. 55416.

Kitchen Glamor, 26770 Grand River Street, Detroit, Mich. 48240.

August Thomsen Corporation, 36 Sea Cliff Avenue, Glen Cove, N.Y. 11542.

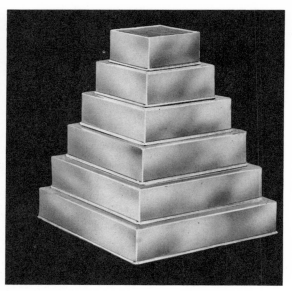

Unusual Cake Pans

TIERED CAKE PANS

Before ordering any of tiered cake pans below which are over 14 inches in size, measure your oven; pan must have 2 inch clearance all around.

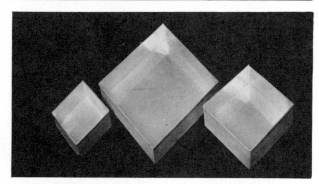

Round Sets

Four pans of 3¼, 5½, 7¼, and 9 inch size.
Four pans of 4, 6, 8, and 10 inch size.
Four pans of 6, 8, 10, and 12 inch size.
Four pans of 5, 7, 9, and 11 inch size.
Also 14 and 16 inch sizes.

Square Sets

Three pans of 4, 6, and 9 inch size.
Three pans of 6, 10, and 14 inch size.
Also 8, 12, and 16 inch sizes.

Rectangular Set

Three pans of 10, 14, and 17½ inch size.

Diamond Set

Three pans of 7, 10, and 15 inch size.

Octagonal Set

Five pans of 6, 8, 10, 12, and 14 inch size.

Heart Set

Three pans of 7, 10, and 13 inch size.

180

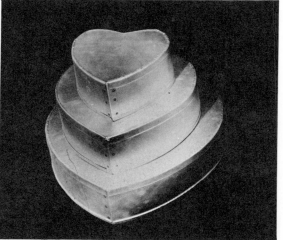

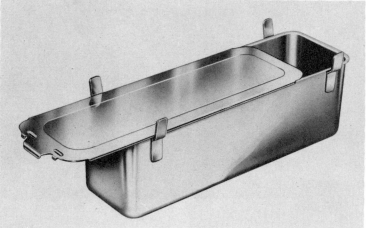

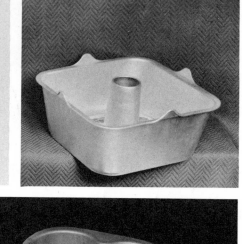

ANGEL CAKE PANS

Long Loaf Pan

About 15½ to 16 inches long. Takes regular angel cake recipe or a package of mix.

Square Pan

About 9 by 4 inches in size. Takes regular angel cake recipe or a package of mix.

Heart Pan

Takes regular angel cake recipe or a package of mix.

Tiered Pan in One Piece

Tiers measure 6, 8, and 10 inches across. Takes regular angel cake recipe or package of mix.

Individual Pans

Each one has his own little cake! Pan is about 4 inches across.

181

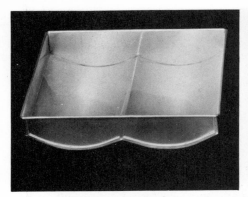

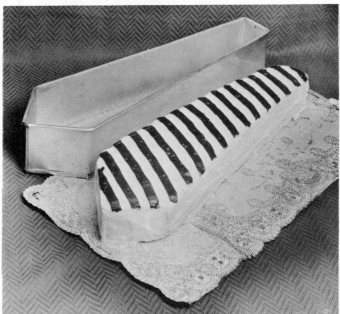

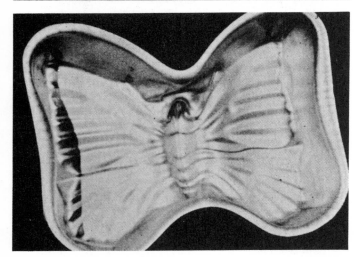

SPECIAL OCCASION PANS

Horseshoe Cake Pan

Nice for anniversaries, going-away parties, etc. It's 13 inches across and 3 inches deep.

Cross Cake Pan

Dramatic and effective for weddings and church festivities. Measures 12 by 17 inches, and is 3 inches deep.

Book Cake Pan

Popular for graduation, confirmation, Bar Mitzvah, christenings, etc. You decorate the book as you wish. Measures 10 by 14 by 3 inches, or 8 by 12 by 3 inches.

Tie Cake Pan

For any man you wish to honor. It measures 17 inches long by 3 inches high.

Butterfly Cake Pan

Ideal for many parties. You decorate the butterfly! Measures 8½ by 6½ by 2¼ inches.

Large Star Cake Pan

Perfect for a holiday cake — one or two layers. It measures 8¾ inches across.

ANIMAL CAKE PANS

Lamb Cake Mold

Everyone loves a lamb cake. See ours and its variations on page 109. Use also for ice cream or salads. Measures 12½ by 7½ inches.

182

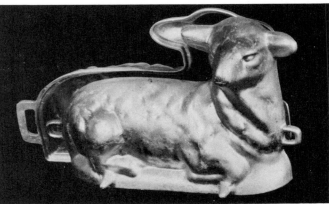

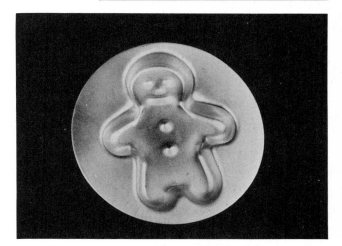

Bunny Cake Mold

Bunnies are favorites of children for birthday parties and Easter. Cover the frosted cake with coconut and tie a ribbon around his neck.

Chicken Cake Mold

Makes a chicken cake to serve at Thanksgiving, Christmas, children's parties, 4-H parties, etc. Measures 5 by 6 by 7 inches.

OTHER SPECIAL PANS

Gingerbread Boy Pan

Your kiddies will love him. He's 9 inches tall, and large enough to serve the family or a birthday party — especially if made in 2 layers.

Christmas Tree Pan Set

Two layer cake pans in the shape of a Christmas tree. An easy festive layer cake for busy days. Frost, then decorate — perhaps with tiny tree balls.

Miniature Layer Cake Pans

Wonderful for individual party cakes. Each measures 4¼ inches, and there are 8 in the set.

Egg Cake Mold

Two-piece cake mold that makes 5 by 7 inch cake. Wonderful for egg cakes or football cakes. You bake the halves separately, ice together as for layer cake, then frost and decorate.

For catalogues on above cake pans and others, see p. 179.

183

INDEX

187